What People Are Sa

Offbeat Philosophers

In *Offbeat Philosophers*, Lawrence Harvey provides a way in to the more 'dissonant' aspects of the work of an eclectic group of philosophers and thinkers. The invitation to take short excursions into that which is unpredictable, idiosyncratic and disruptive in thinkers such as Max Stirner, Donna Haraway, Paul Rée, Emmanuel Levinas and Jalal al-Din Rumi, is a compelling re-orientation towards the margins of much conventional curricula and pedagogy. Highly engaging, educative and readable, the book will appeal simultaneously to readers and teachers already taken to wandering off the beaten track as well as those looking for confidence to take that first step.

Dr Rebekah Howes, Senior Lecturer in the Department of Philosophy, Religions, and Liberal Arts at the University of Winchester (UK)

Lawrence invites the reader to hear, then to listen to, then to become enraptured with, and finally to join in with a different philosophical rhythm than the manifold conformities that prevail in the stultified world of cultural education. These different beats are pedagogical; they are grounded in his own teaching and learning with students over many years, something at which he is gifted and inspiring. His readings are provocative, challenging, and fearless. Expect to be moved, but not to know in which ways until the experience is under way. The themes may seem familiar, but the way Lawrence plays them to us are not. Do not read this book seeking to master it. It does not seek to master you. Just let it play...

Professor Nigel Tubbs, Professor of Philosophy and Education and author *Socrates on Trial*; *God, Education, and Modern Metaphysics*; *Philosophy and Modern Liberal Arts*; and *History of Western Philosophy*

In this delightful anthology, Lawrence Harvey presents ten offbeat philosophers. The crowning glory of this work is his ability to snapshot interesting and offbeat facts from the life of each philosopher whilst enigmatically capturing the essence of their thought. The result is a well-researched, witty, and engaging tour through a range of philosophers exploring topics as diverse as the ego, time, the soul, God, poetry, art, cyborgs, and mysticism. For anyone who is interested in philosophy but wants to diverge from the limited narrative of the mainstream canon, this work is a gem that dares to be different.

Tara Baker, Head of Religious Studies, Peter Symonds College, Hampshire, UK

Offbeat Philosophers serves as a warm, lively, and accessible introduction to some of the most interesting philosophical minds. Harvey casts a deserving light on the work of these eccentric thinkers whose ideas have occupied only the fringes of mainstream philosophy. Those new to philosophy will find themselves engaged by strikingly thought-provoking theories, whilst those acquainted with the philosophical tradition shall come to realise just how influential these "off-beat" philosophers were to the giants of the canon.

Callum Webb, Balliol College, University of Oxford

Offbeat Philosophers

Thinkers Who Played a Different Tune

Offbeat Philosophers

Thinkers Who Played a Different Tune

Dr Lawrence Harvey

IFF
BOOKS

London, UK
Washington, DC, USA

CollectiveInk

First published by iff Books, 2024
iff Books is an imprint of Collective Ink Ltd.,
Unit 11, Shepperton House, 89 Shepperton Road, London, N1 3DF
office@collectiveinkbooks.com
www.collectiveinkbooks.com
www.iff-books.com

For distributor details and how to order please visit the 'Ordering' section on our website.

Text copyright: Lawrence Harvey 2023

ISBN: 978 1 80341 614 4
978 1 80341 631 1 (ebook)
Library of Congress Control Number: 2023942930

A CIP catalogue record for this book is available from the British Library.

Design: Lapiz Digital Services

UK: Printed and bound by CPI Group (UK) Ltd, Croydon, CR0 4YY
Printed in North America by CPI GPS partners

We operate a distinctive and ethical publishing philosophy in
all areas of our business, from our global network of authors to
production and worldwide distribution.

"What assistance can one find in the fight against habit? Try the opposite!"

— Epictetus, *Discourses*, 1.27.4

I am greatly indebted to my philosophy and liberal arts students; their input in terms of stimulating debates and lively discussions gives shape and form to much that is contained herein.

Contents

Preface

This collection of philosophical portraits provides insights into thinkers who played by a different tune. Often labouring on the margins of mainstream philosophy, each thinker herein offers a new perspective unhindered by the accepted norms or conventions of their day. Each portrait is followed by post-reading questions for the reader to ponder — after all, is not 'philosophy' *always already* a verb?

How might we define 'offbeat'? Let us start with a list of synonyms: bizarre, unusual, idiosyncratic, unconventional, plain weird ... bohemian perhaps, outré, freaky, 'far-out' even. Originally a musical term, it refers to *not* following the standard beat. Digging a little deeper we encounter the term 'syncopation' which relates to an array of rhythms played together generating that which is 'offbeat'. In this way, the regular rhythmic flow is disrupted with accents and stresses occurring out of step with the expected norms.

The musical metaphor is apt in the present context given that the philosophers in this short anthology all play to what might be termed a different tune — one that serves to disrupt and unsettle the fixity of rhythmic thought.

Many of the portraits herein are developed from studies I have published elsewhere; a list of which is appended. Rather than using formal references, I have opted to maximise readability by attaching a selected bibliography for each key thinker and the associated academics cited.

***

Lawrence Harvey
Northwood, The Isle of Wight

Introduction

'When we teach, we learn' — words often attributed to the Roman philosopher and statesman, Seneca the Younger. There is perhaps an obvious sense in which this statement is true; one must, one imagines, both know and refine one's understanding when playing the pedagogue. And yet I would suggest that there is a more subtle sense in which Seneca's words ring true. To my mind, teaching is always in some sense a dialogue; a space within which the absolutism of the teacher gives way to an open and creative dialogue. In the words of the ethicist, Emmanuel Levinas, that which is 'said' gives way to an interchange of 'saying'. To the hard-pressed lecturer or student attempting to cover a prescribed syllabus, such ideals might sound somewhat indulgent. Still, in my experience, it is often within the context of such discussions, often enacted on the margins of that prescribed, that truly innovative and reciprocal learning takes place.

Much of the focus in this anthology stems from my teaching within the strictures of set syllabi. Yet it 'stems' thus at a tangent. That is to say, most of the thinkers engaged in this work were not posited by an exam board or rubber-stamped by a validating body. The educational 'beat' plays to such bodies — there is little to be gained by bemoaning such necessities here. However, the thinkers herein represent an edifying dissonance; that is, they offer alternative perspectives which challenge and provoke. It is such thinkers that I have invited into seminars and discussions to sound a different tune; and often it has been within the ensuing discord that the learning truly comes to life. It is the provocative nature of such offbeat thinkers that ignites the debate and scorches preconceptions — thankfully, my own included, *docendo discimus* ('by teaching, we learn').

3

I am all too aware that the thinkers in this anthology do not represent an inclusive snapshot of alternative philosophers. No doubt, the choices that govern inclusion herein were subject to my own interests, preoccupations and personal biases. But having said this, what is represented here is a diverse and thematically interwoven tapestry of offbeat thinkers who provoke us to examine our world in radically different ways. The questions that follow each chapter are an open invitation to join in the debate and perhaps think *other-wise*.

The anthology opens with Max Stirner (1806–1856) who boldly proclaimed, 'For me, you are nothing but my food...' This egoistic call to arms issues from the one book of significance which the now uncelebrated German philosopher published in his lifetime; a work which Marx and Engels thought so radically unhinged that it warranted a section-by-section critique in *The German Ideology* (1846). Prefiguring the likes of Nietzsche, Stirner derided God and the truth in the name of the bellicose ego which is both 'creator and creature'. It is doubtful if there could be a more vociferous challenge to contemporary ethical ideals.

What is time? Is death an impossibility? Is time travel possible? In Chapter Two, we explore J. W. Dunne's (1875–1949) responses to such questions. Drawing upon his analysis of what he took to be precognitive dreams, Dunne argued that we have a rather skewed view of time and thereby labour under the illusion that time amounts to a linear constraint. What he offers is a freedom from such temporal shackles, wherein one can play the keyboard of one's life unencumbered by time's passing. In addition, he forwards a 'proof' of immortality and prophesies that the hand of a Great Conductor (God?) will become manifest, conducting the symphony of all creation.

In her *Manifesto*, Donna Haraway (b. 1944) proclaimed: 'I would rather be a cyborg than a goddess'. Chapter Three explores the implications of this rather enigmatic proclamation. For Haraway, the breach of binary oppositions and essentialising boundaries embodied in the image of the cyborg serves to shake us free from a stultifying essentialism. Defining labels, truths and preconceived identities wither under the cyborg's steely gaze — both God(s) and Goddess(es) ceding the ground to the playful hybridity of the cyborg. Crucially, we might ask, are we all already cyborgs? Does the tech in our pockets mark the beginnings of the post-human age? Moreover, in the name of identity, does the reassurance of a fundamental 'essence' or (human) nature blind us to broader and more ethical affinities? Such are the questions that Haraway tenders, but always at a playful tangent.

Chapter Four shifts the focus to the realm of art and poetry. Therein the somewhat schismatic work of T. E Hulme (1883–1917) is outlined. Something of a hellraiser with an appetite for fighting and epic walks, Hulme formulated a philosophical rationale for the ever-protean modernist aesthetic. Although now something of a peripheral philosopher, his metaphysics and aesthetics influenced key modernist figures such as Ezra Pound and T. S. Eliot. Carrying the only copy of his final manuscript, the pro-war Hulme was blown to pieces by an artillery shell in Belgium. Yet despite this untimely end, his radical poetics influenced the aesthetics of a generation.

Are you two substances — body and soul, mind and matter in motion? If so, how are these two radically different substances supposed to interact with each other? How is it that your thoughts, your wants and your desires animate your body? As outlined in Chapter Five, such were the perplexing questions that Nicolas Malebranche (1638–1715) attempted to answer. Following in the wake of Descartes, but sensitive to his shortfalls, Malebranche offered a radically offbeat solution for something as simple as moving one's hand. Wherein lies the cause of your hand moving? Not where you think…

In Chapter Six, one of our most intuitive and vital preconceptions is challenged by the German philosopher, Paul Rée (1849–1901). Despite societal and moral constraints, and taking on board the extent to which we are shaped by our genetic inheritance, most of us believe we have a degree of free will, at least at some fundamental level. Are you not free to skip a line of this text or glance up from the page? As the guru of liberty, Jean-Paul Sartre (1905–1980) might have put it, isn't our life punctuated by existential choices, the nature of which gives shape, form and meaning to who and what we are? Moreover, even in the most extreme situations, do we not hold others accountable for their actions on the basis that their choices are, at root, free? Wielding the cold scalpel of empiricism, Rée cuts away our intuitive preconceptions and associated moral niceties, laying bare the consequences of causal necessity. In short, he concludes, we are as free as the celestial bodies in their orbits, we are as free as the ripe apple that falls from the bough — that is to say, we are *not* free at all and, for good or ill, no one is ever responsible for their actions.

Humans are those unique animals that value art, whether lines upon a page, brush strokes upon a canvas, or an admix of harmony, melody and rhythm. In light of its universality, why do we value art? Is it because of its ability to express the emotions of the artist? Or rather, is it of value because it can stir the emotions in the sensitive reader, listener or observer; does it 'speak to the heart' as it were? Could it be that the value of art lies in its transformative nature; in its ability, that is, to open up vistas of being which lie dormant or untapped? Setting aside such ideals, is art merely an object of entertainment; a means by which we can distract ourselves and escape from the humdrum? To strike an even more cynical note, is art that which art institutions dictate to be art and thus of real value? Does value in this sense reside in conformity to a social construct we unwittingly consume? When it comes to art, the question of value is, to say the least, nebulous. In Chapter Seven, the British philosopher and art critic, Clive Bell (1881–1964), offers forth what he took to be clarity regarding this much-debated question. According to Bell, value lies in what he terms 'significant form' — a feature of art which allows the sensitive observer to lift the veil of perception and glimpse the essential nature of reality itself.

In Chapter Eight we encounter the work of a remarkable woman who directly challenged the work of Descartes. Through a seven-year correspondence with the French philosopher, Princess Elisabeth of Bohemia (1618–1680) meticulously critiqued Cartesian thought, most notably laying bare the problem of causal interaction between the mind and the body. As outlined in Chapter Five, Malebranche tried to rectify this philosophical difficulty. However, it was Elisabeth of Bohemia who directly deconstructed the inner workings of Descartes' dualistic account of the self. Hold your hand before your eyes — move your fingers. Supposing your mind to be immaterial, how is possible that this immaterial substance moves your physical fingers? Upon reflection, something quite miraculous appears to have happened. Yet setting aside the miraculous, hasn't something quite impossible occurred? It was Elisabeth of Bohemia who opened Descartes' eyes to this deficit in his thinking and offered her own radical speculations.

Is Western philosophy a form of disguised conflict? Is the so-called 'love of wisdom' wedded to war? According to the ethicist Emmanuel Levinas (1906–1995), the answer to these questions is an unsettling 'yes'. In Chapter Nine, the reasoning behind this radical claim is outlined. So too is Levinas' bold claim that, despite the ubiquity of conflict, we are already conditioned by a profound encounter which is, at root, pacific. In other words, our very being is dependent upon a primordial passivity which marks out the very condition of what it is to be human. Connecting these threads of reasoning, if philosophy is characterised by conflict, it is a conflict which is only possible because of a passivity or ethical encounter which precedes it. As abstract as this might sound, Levinas challenges the working rationale of Western philosophy and offers, in its place, an appeal to a form of ethics which precedes any intellectual call to arms.

Looking at one's life and situating it within the infinity of space and time, one might be driven to conclude that one's existence is tantamount to a drop in a vast and unfathomable ocean. The philosopher-poet Jalal al-Din Rumi (1207–1273) invites us to think differently; what if you are the entire ocean in a drop? In the wake of a chance encounter with a wandering mystic or dervish, Rumi was a thinker for whom the philosophical beat changed radically. Abandoning the tenets of scholastic sobriety, he became a mystical philosopher-poet who, even today, challenges us to think otherwise. In Chapter Ten, we encounter his offbeat critique of what he takes to be the pretensions of rational philosophy. And yet within this critique resides a tangential engagement with some of the fundamental questions interrogated in academic philosophy. For example, contrary to the principle of excluded middle, is it possible to be *both* free and determined at the same time? In a manner we might parallel to Wittgenstein offering to 'shew' the philosopher-fly out of its linguistic bottle, Rumi invites us to reappraise our binary logic and thereby escape the prison house of traditional thought. It is perhaps such an emancipation that the text to hand gestures towards.

CHAPTER I

Max Stirner: Egoism

"For me you are nothing but — my food..."

In May 1856, the German philosopher, Max Stirner (1806–1856), was stung on the neck by an insect. As a result, he developed a fever and died the following month. In this unfortunate manner, Stirner entered the pantheon of dead philosophers. And yet despite dwelling in the shadows of this edifice, Stirner's influence on the trajectory of modern philosophy has been significant, if largely unsung. As the critic, Michael Levenson, puts it, Stirner was something of 'an intellectual oddity, [...] the author of one book of consequence, which appeared without warning, stirred immediate controversy, and then fell into obscurity'.

Stirner was born in Bayreuth, Germany, in October 1806. In the autumn of 1826, he began a period of study within the faculty of philosophy at the University of Berlin. It was these formative years that were to profoundly affect his later polemical work. His thought was shaped by a reaction against the dialectical method as set forth by Hegel. From 1818 until his death in 1831, Hegel was a professor of philosophy at the University of Berlin. Stirner attended the maestro's lecturers, and yet instead of passively consuming his mentor's ideas, he began to formulate a radical ontology diametrically opposed to that set down by Hegel. In a nutshell, Hegelian thought is founded upon the subordination of the individual ego to an abstract absolute. For Stirner, this process of subordination was anathema.

In marked opposition to his Young Hegelian brethren (a group of German intellectuals also sometimes known as the Hegelian Left), Stirner sought an ontological paradigm devoid of any lingering appeal to an abstract absolute or residual sense of otherness. To this end, he invoked a radical sense of what he termed 'ownness' or egoism. Stirner outlined this philosophical egoism in his magnum opus, *The Ego and Its Own* (1844). Therein, he argued that the all-powerful ego is unique and ontologically sovereign and hence we should not defer to some external prop. 'Turn to yourselves rather than to your gods or idols', as he put it. 'Bring out from yourselves what is in you, bring it to the light, bring it yourselves to revelation.' According to Stirner's often playful argument, this state of uniqueness does not in any sense expunge a sense of corporality by way of a paradoxical appeal to idealism. On the contrary, it is Stirner's contention that, once released from a state of alienation, the ego falls in love with its 'corporeal self'. Within the terms of this narcissism, the ego takes pleasure in itself as a living flesh-and-blood entity. Thus, the peerless ego *is* corporeal and as such does not exist in relation to any incorporeal essence. It would seem to follow that concepts such as 'man' are insufficient inasmuch as such concepts or 'fixed ideas' emanate from the ego itself as incorporeal creations. Mindful of the seeming self-contradiction, Stirner concludes that the ego does not correspond to 'man' but rather to 'un-man' or *unmensch*. In what Stiner terms 'blunt words', an 'un-man' is a man 'who does not correspond to the *concept* of man, as the inhuman is something human which is not conformed to the *concept* of the human'. The concept of man is thus repudiated as a defunct essence or truth. For Stirner, all such truths are to be cast aside: 'As long as you believe in the truth, you do not believe in yourself, [...] you are more than the truth, which is nothing at all before you'. Hence it is that Stirner valorised the individual over and above the truth or any extrinsic form; a philosophical theme that would come to dominate subsequent Nietzschean and existentialist thought. Yet instead of attempting to affirm in the face of vacuity or reaching for some form of authenticity within the nothingness of being, Stirner embraces the nihilistic consequences; 'I do not love the world, for I *annihilate* it, as I annihilate myself'. Thus, for thinkers such as Albert Camus (1913–1960), it was Stirner rather than Nietzsche that epitomised the spirit of absurdity. According to Camus, Stirner was an 'egoistic-monarch' who embodied the vacuous state of modern being — his nihilism being satisfied.

Yet what of the consequences of such unabashed egoism? R. W. K. Paterson paints a vivid portrait of all that is negative and destructive: 'On the grim, predatory features of the ruthless egoist Stirner has etched the hollow, dissipated features of the uncaring nihilist'. Within ethical terms, Stirner's egoism can thus be construed as disastrous. Indeed, it is Stirner's contention that the Other is an object of consumption: 'For me you are nothing but — my food'. In this manner, Stirner's egoism boils down to the claim that the Other is a means to an end — a pawn in what amounts to an insidious game of egocentric advancement. Even what appear to be unselfish appeals to the Other are veiled or oblique manifestations of the egocentric will. For example, it is Stirner's contention that love and/or altruism are, at root, sentiments motivated by an egocentric volition. The altruistic act is thus one that the ego believes will be of benefit to the Self. In this manner, Stirner's brand of egoism is party to a denial of the Other; a denial vigorously contested by influential ethicists such as Emmanuel Levinas.

The full force of Stirner's polemic can be measured against the time and effort which Marx and Engels devoted to critiquing it. And yet less than a month after the first publication of *The Ego and Its Own*, Engels voiced his enthusiasm in a letter to Marx: 'whatever we will on behalf of some idea, we have first to make our cause personal, egoistic [...] it is equally from egoism that we are communists'. In addition, Engels claimed that Stirner was right to reject the 'Man' of Feuerbach since his Man is derived from God. Under the guiding influence of Marx, Engels modified this positive evaluation — the greater part of *The German Ideology* (1846) constituting a point-by-point critique of Stirner's text. With unbridled scorn, Marx likens Stirner to Don Quixote's squire, Sancho Panza: 'Saint Sancho attacks the halo (the windmill) of existing power'. Furthermore, 'Saint Max' is accused of substituting an active bourgeois egoism for a 'bragging egoism in agreement with itself'. However, as some academics have attempted to establish, that other herald of the modern spirit, Friedrich Nietzsche (1844–1900), was, albeit tacitly, far from critical of Stirner. In fact, some academics have gone as far as to argue that Nietzsche plagiarised Stirner — an act that would, if true, enthrone Stirner as the duped precursor of continental philosophy.

But setting aside this debate, it is clear that Stirner's work lays bare the enduring estrangement that haunts the modern world; more so than Nietzsche, more so than the subsequent existential philosophers perhaps, Stirner sounds this abiding discord. Today, his unnerving brand of egoism can be construed as embodying an extreme position against which ethicists are still attempting to find recourse. To use Marx and Engels's sardonic label, ethical harmony must, it seems, take into account the acerbic vigour of Saint Max's stark and disquieting cacophony.

***

Food for thought:

- Are we at root more selfish than we might at first imagine?
- Does a veneer of selflessness dupe us into repressing an unpalatable truth?
- Is a selfless act ever possible?

- Are so-called selfless acts always underpinned by an unspoken egoism?
- Despite societal norms and customary niceties, should we *always* look out for our own self-interest?
- If we are brutally honest with ourselves, are others merely 'our food' in the game of life?
- Is rampant egoism an ethical abhorrence we should dismiss out of hand or an uncomfortable reality that warrants serious ethical reflection?
- Do we have an 'essence'?
- Or to put it another way, is there a sense in which we conform to a 'fixed idea' or concept, perhaps despite ourselves?
- To what extent are you self-creative or formulated?
- Are you at the helm of your 'ship of life' or are you a passenger?
- Is it healthy to face the so-called vacuity or nothingness of being? Can we really live without the reassurance of external truths?
- Or are there external essences or truths against which we *should* measure our being?
- Does total freedom entail nihilism?
- As Dostoyevsky once put it, if God does not exist, is everything permitted?
- Far from losing oneself in the beloved, is love selfish to the core?
- Is excessive criticism a form of tacit endorsement?

CHAPTER II

J. W. Dunne: Time and Immortality

"The Hand of a Great Conductor will become manifest, and we shall discover that we are taking part in a Symphony of All Creation..."

As Augustine famously put it, we think we know what time is until someone asks us for a definition. Although labouring on the offbeat peripheries of mainstream academic philosophy and physics, the Anglo-Irish philosopher, J. W. Dunne (1875–1949), attempted to define the ineffable with his own highly influential theory of time. In the words of the playwright and novelist J. B. Priestley, 'those of us who are Time-haunted owe him an enormous debt'.

John William Dunne was the son of an Irishman, General Sir John Hart Dunne, and his English wife, Julia Elizabeth Dunne. Serving as a trooper and infantry officer, he fought in the Boer War. Like Wittgenstein, he was also originally an aeronautical engineer, designing early tailless swept-wing aircraft — his designs being secretly tested by the War Office as early as 1907. As officially witnessed by Orville Wright, Dunne's D.5 was certified as the first aircraft to achieve aerodynamic stability in flight. This unassuming eclectic also wrote children's books and was something of an authority on angling, credited with inventing a new approach to dry-fly fishing. And yet it is his challenge to the so-called dogma of chronological unidimensional time which marks Dunne out as a philosopher of note; his work constituting, as he put himself, 'an extremely cautious reconnaissance in a rather novel direction'.

A seemingly precocious child, Dunne questioned his nurse as to the true nature of time. She obliged, explaining how we are travelling from yesterday to today and are moving onwards to tomorrow. Unconvinced, the young John William asked her, 'which did she mean was time: yesterday, today and tomorrow: or the time which it took us to travel from the one to the other?' From that point onwards, Dunne was unable to rid himself of the conviction that time flowed; but without, as he later put it, replicating 'Newton's error of supposing that the "flow" was "without reference to anything external"'.

These early thoughts coalesced into a full-fledged theory in 1927 when Dunne published what became an unlikely bestseller, *An Experiment with Time*. Therein, Dunne outlined the central tenets of his philosophy: Precognitivism and Serialism. The former idea stemmed from a series of supposedly precognitive dreams that Dunne experienced, many of which were mundane in nature and soberly recorded. In the wake of such dreams, Dunne 'did not feel he was about to become a prophet' nor did he take leave of his rational faculty and ascribe such puzzling experiences to astral wanderings, telepathy or clairvoyance. Buoyed by the corroborating testimonies of others, he inquired as to whether it was possible that such phenomena were not abnormal, but normal. As he asked, were dreams 'composed of images of past experience and *images of future experience blended together in approximately equal proportions*?' This line of inquiry led to a radical and influential reformulation of the concept of Time itself. It was just conceivable, he argued, that 'the universe was, after all, really stretched out in Time' — the 'lop-sided view' we have of it, 'a view with the "future" part unaccountably missing, cut off from the growing "past" part by a travelling "present" moment — was due to a purely mentally imposed barrier which existed only when we were awake'.

Distancing himself from any charges of occultism, Dunne developed his notion of Serial Time (or Serialism) as a means to rationalise this precognitive vision, armour-plating his account with appeals to mathematics, science and psychology. Despite its complexities, he claimed that his central thesis was 'considerably easier to understand than are, say, the rules of Contract Bridge'. With a nod to both Einstein and burgeoning quantum theory, Dunne argued that there was no place for the individual observer within the orthodox scientific paradigm of his day. By way of redress, he argued that whilst we experience time in a chronological manner when awake, there is, by necessity, a higher dimension of Time which serves to frame the lower — a time that *times* the linear passage of Time so to speak. Happy to invite into the equation that bugbear of philosophers, the infinite regress, he argued that if Time 'passes or grows or accumulates or expends itself or does anything whatsoever except stand rigid and changeless before a Time-fixed observer, there must be another Time which times that activity [...] and so on in an apparent series to infinity'. In this manner, Dunne added what he termed a sensory centre of observation to the fourth dimension of Time, beckoning in its wake a seemingly infinite series of self-observing selves.

In light of Dunne's systematic study of flight, this serial schema can perhaps be metaphorically mapped onto the vantage point of the pilot. Whilst by terrestrial day we move forward in time (one-second-per-second), from the lofty perspective of sleep, we are freed from the fetters of linear temporality. In other words, from the vantage point of eternity, we are able to travel both forwards and backwards, looking down, as it were, upon our alter-ego, that plodding time-bound pedestrian labouring within a set chronology. Flying at a still higher altitude, another pilot (or serial observer) looks down upon the first and so on and so forth in perpetuity. Interestingly, prior to the outbreak of the First World War, Dunne helped facilitate H. G. Wells' first flight in an aeroplane. And yet, unlike the author of *The Time Machine*, Dunne set aside the need for fanciful mechanical contraptions: open to all, sleep being the medium of temporal liberty.

In J. B. Priestley's estimation, Dunne's *An Experiment with Time* was 'one of the most fascinating, most curious, and perhaps the most important books' of the age. Priestley's early enthusiasm for Dunne's philosophy gave shape and form to his seminal time play, *Time and the Conways* (1937). The First Act, set in 1919, depicts the joys of a post-war family reunion. In the Second Act, set in Priestley's present, the self-same characters appear, albeit twisted by time and disenchanted with their lives. Act Three marks a return to 1919, a return tempered by the precognitive vision of future anguish and disillusionment. There is even a direct reference to Dunne's text in the play: 'No... it's hard to explain [...] there's a book I'll lend you — read it in the train. But the point is, now, at this moment, or any other moment, we're only a cross-section of our real selves'. But more than this, in Priestley's play, Dunne's Serialism is peddled as something akin to an ethical panacea: 'You know, I believe half our trouble now is because we think Time's ticking our lives away. That's why we snatch and grab and hurt each other [...] as if we were all in a panic on a sinking ship'.

Yet despite influencing such literary greats as James Joyce, J. R. R. Tolkien, W. B. Yeats, Jorge Luis Borges, and T. S. Eliot to name but a few, Dunne's philosophy has not endured. In spite of stripping away any suggestion of the miraculous with his hard-nosed reason and complex diagrammatical illustrations, his research into precognitive dreams is at best anecdotal. Moreover, Dunne's invocation of an infinite regress is often interpreted as an act of ad hocism perpetrated by an amateur philosopher delighting in the role of *l'enfant terrible*. As J. B. Priestley put it: 'Just as the medieval map makers, once they had left behind them a known coastline, filled in the great blank spaces with dragons and other monsters, Dunne rushed in his regress'. This said, Dunne also rather paradoxically invokes a 'superlative general observer' — this observer being a final term set within a series, which, by the very nature of its internal logic, can abide no such final term. With a mind to the self-contradiction, Dunne concedes that he has wandered from his main task into 'what appears to be a region for exploration by the theologian'.

In later texts such as *The New Immortality* (1938) and *Nothing Dies* (1940), Dunne explored this latent aspect of his philosophy, developing a theory of serial immortality; at the higher levels of self-observation, one cannot be anything other than immortal he argued. Further expounding his ideas in a lecture with piano accompaniment recorded by the BBC in 1937, Dunne argued that whilst Observer 1 (the wakeful self) might be able to play the chromatic scale, *andante*, and Observer 2 (the dreaming self) ranges across the keyboard playing discords, *crescendo*, it is only the Observer *at* infinity that can play the individual notes (the events of a 'lifetime of human experience') with symphonic harmony. 'Think of what you can do! The whole range of musical composition lies before you, and this with an instrument, the keyboard of which is a lifetime of human experience of every description.' Dunne even went as far as to proclaim that he was scientifically certain that the 'Hand of a Great Conductor will become manifest, and we shall discover that we are taking part in a Symphony of All Creation' — all of which prompted H. G. Wells to comment that his aberrant friend had lost all sense of proportion.

Even though modern thought has falsified many of his broader and more offbeat claims, there is no denying the influence of Dunne's pioneering philosophy of time. As J. B. Priestley put it — Dunne 'has still to be praised and honoured as one of our great originals and liberators. I should like to think there was some way of conveying these thanks and a loud and affectionate *Bravo* to his Observer Two or Three'.

***

Food for thought:

- Do we think we know what time is until someone asks us for a definition?
- The ancient Greek Sophist, Antiphon, stated that time is a concept or measure, not a substance or reality. Does time really exist?
- Could it be that the universe is stretched out *in* time and the skewed view we have of it, with the 'future' part missing, is due to a mentally imposed barrier?
- Are we harried by a sense that time is ticking our lives away and thus, 'snatch and grab and hurt each other [...] as if we were all in a panic on a sinking ship'?
- Does time have definitive topological or geometrical form? Should we think of time as linear? Does time travel from past to present in a straight line, as it were? If so, is there just one 'stream' of time or many? Or is time perhaps cyclical — does it travel in a circular manner? Is time thus better construed as a wheel? Would this entail a process of 'eternal recurrence' or a revisiting of one's past?
- Are our concepts of the past and future real? When time passes, one's present becomes one's past, and one's future becomes one's present. Hence, if we only encounter the present 'in time', is that present the only reality?
- Is time infinite or eternal? Does time have no beginning nor end — is it infinite? Or was there a point at which time began and hence a point at which it might end?
- Does an analysis of time entail immortality as Dunne suggests?
- The so-called 'quiet Beatle', George Harrison, once stated that it is the here and now that is vital. Why? Because there is no past and there is no future. Is there wisdom or folly in this assertion?

CHAPTER III

Donna Haraway: The Rise of the Cyborgs

"I would rather be a cyborg than a goddess."

Reflecting upon the oddity of her position within the socio-economic framework of the twentieth century, Donna Haraway once described herself as an Irish Catholic girl whose PhD in biology was made possible by 'Sputnik's impact on US national science-education policy'. As she elaborated, 'I have a body and a mind as much constructed by the post-Second World War arms race and cold war as by the women's movement'. Yet, instead of producing a loyal American technocrat, Haraway became a dissident prophet of the posthuman cyborg, a notional hybrid which purported to offer an escape from delimiting socio-cultural gender hierarchies. For Haraway, the cyborg breaches boundaries and, as such, offers heady fusions replete with dangerous possibilities. Within the protean framework of her postmodern feminism, the cyborg is representative of binary dissolution. Old dualisms, such as the mechanistic and the organic, the human and the animal, the physical and the ideal are challenged through the ironic interplay of the incompatible.

Donna Haraway was born in Denver, Colorado in 1944. Her mother was of working-class Irish Catholic descent; suffering chronic ill health, she died of a heart attack when Haraway was sixteen years old. Her father was a sportswriter working for *The Denver Post*. According to Haraway, he was something of a logophile and father and daughter would discuss their shared fascination of the written word over dinner. With her father, Haraway attended seventy-odd baseball games a year. By her own admission, she also 'played basketball with lots of passion, if mediocre talent'. Her formative education was at St Mary's Academy in Cherry Hills Village, Colorado — her mother's friend, a nun, being the principal of the Catholic high school. According to Haraway, her early years were shaped by the pervasive influence of Catholicism; yet despite seriously considering entering the convent, doubts relating to the proof of God's existence crept in when she was ten or eleven. Playfully espousing (and 'exposing') Nietzsche, she would later proclaim, 'god' is dead and so is the 'goddess'.

Haraway's formative years were also shaped by experiencing opposing ideologies. She encountered 'McCarthyism from the point of view of an Irish Catholic family that was anti-Communist and convinced by Cold War ideology'. On the other hand, she would listen to the rhetoric of the parish priest, charged with taking the children's confession. He was a former Belgian missionary in the People's Republic of China and would 'scare the living hell' out of his flock by claiming that the West was going to lose the fight against world communism. Why? Because, he claimed, the children of the USSR and 'Red China' were morally superior, ideologically committed and far less decadent — a claim that seemed to deeply impress the young Haraway. One could perhaps argue that this formative grounding in very convincing but contrary ideologies went some way to shaping Haraway's later emphasis on the play of ironic contradictions as a means by which to circumvent epistemic polarities.

Having gained a full scholarship from the Brettcher Foundation, Haraway studied at Colorado College, a liberal arts institution, graduating in 1966 with a major in zoology and minors in English literature and philosophy. Upon graduation, she moved to France and studied the philosophy of science at the Faculté des Sciences, Université de Paris, and evolutionary philosophy and theology at the Fondation

Teilhard de Chardin, Paris. At Yale graduate school, Haraway's dissertation supervisor was the British ecologist, G. Evelyn Hutchinson, who, as she puts it, 'made it a habit in his life to support women who were mildly to extremely heterodox'. Her dissertation interrogated the use of metaphors in experimental biology; according to Haraway it was 'written under the spell' of Thomas Kuhn's work on incommensurability and vying paradigms. Despite her methodological affinities with the deconstructive method, Haraway did not encounter the work of thinkers such as Jacques Derrida, Harold Bloom, Peter Brooks or Paul de Man until she was working at the John Hopkins University, Baltimore. Asked if she felt a sense of recognition when she became acquainted with such thinkers, she replied, 'No, they were on another planet as far as I was concerned'. Given the manner in which she uses deconstruction within the context of postcolonial feminism, Haraway seems to have found the work of writers such Gayatri Spivak more inspirational than that proffered by the so-called American deconstructionists. Moreover, rather than the French poststructuralists, Haraway was initially influenced by the work of philosophers such as Alfred North Whitehead, Charles Peirce and Martin Heidegger. Often described as a postmodernist feminist, she has made significant impacts within fields as diverse as developmental biology, primatology, posthumanism and eco-feminism. In the 1980s, Haraway published groundbreaking essays including *A Manifesto for Cyborgs: Science, Technology, and Socialist Feminism* (1985) and *Situated Knowledges: The Science Question in Feminism as a Site of Discourse on the Privilege of Partial Perspective* (1988).

Focusing on the former and perhaps most well-known text, what exactly is a cyborg? The word is itself a hybrid term or portmanteau derived from 'cybernetic' and 'organism' — it fuses that which is organic and technology. Broadly construed, the cyborg can be seen as representative of the growing interconnectedness which exists between humans and technology. In a sense, we are all cyborgs given the ever-deepening fusion of technology and biofunction. Thus, as Haraway puts it, the cyborg is a 'hybrid of machine and organism, a creature of social reality as well as a creature of fiction'. Haraway invokes the image of the cyborg so as to challenge ridged polarities, binaries and attendant hierarchies which, as she sees it, serve to perpetuate the myth of the one Truth, the 'natural' or the *telos*. According to Haraway, traditional feminist identity politics is complicit with such an essentialising or totalising narrative. Playfully echoing the Marxist call to action, the *Manifesto* offers an alternative path shaped by an oxymoronic 'myth' which embodies contradictions and the incompatible. In short, it is a provocation to think otherwise.

Existing in a post-gender world, Haraway argues that the cyborg 'has no truck with bisexuality, pre-oedipal symbiosis, unalienated labour, or other seductions to organic wholeness through a final appropriation of all the powers of the parts into a higher unity'. Herein, Haraway is challenging the Hegelian dream of a dialectical synthesis wherein all contradictions resolve into an absolute truth. Rejecting both original and dialectical unity, the cyborg is committed to partiality, perversity and irony; thereby subverting the organic wholes which give shape and form to the 'antagonistic dualisms' of Western philosophy. To be specific, dualisms such as male/female, right/wrong, truth/illusion, free/determined, self/other, etc. compete for the mantle of truth and are thus complicit in a discourse of domination. In stark contrast, Haraway's cyborg subverts the Truth and any sense of a unified or essential human subject able to apprehend the said *Truth*. Within such terms, cyborgs are devoid of the will to produce any totalising theories. Instead, they enact and embody an intimate experience of both the construction and deconstruction of boundaries. Along with patriarchy, the dialectics of colonialism, essentialism and naturalism are thus challenged by the cyborg — what is tendered is a 'way out of the maze of dualisms'. In this way, the *Cyborg Manifesto* marks a Kuhnian shift from the shards of polemic modernism to the ironic praxis of postmodernism.

The *Cyborg Manifesto* was a controversial and divisive text from the off. Indeed, its publication history was shaped by a critical schism — the East Coast Collective of the American *Socialist Review* deemed it politically naïve, anti-feminist and bereft of critique. However, the Berkeley Collective rejected this evaluation and facilitated its publication. There has also been much debate as to Haraway's style of expression. For example, whilst commenting on the ubiquity of the *Manifesto* within the humanities and social sciences, Jackie Orr has pointed out that many students find the text 'curiously relevant but somewhat impenetrable'. Yet this opaque method is intentional for Haraway is endeavouring to avoid any sedimentation in a new epistemic perspective. That is to say, her texts are deliberately open to numerous and sometimes contradictory readings via the 'serious play' of irony. For Haraway, irony embraces contradictions and thereby frustrates the march of truth discourses. Playfully debunking binary logic and the law of excluded middle, irony holds 'incompatible things together because both or all are necessary and true'. Cyborgs personify such fabricated hybridisation and Haraway's mode of expression is likewise chimeric. All of which is perhaps somewhat infuriating for those schooled in the analytic tradition of philosophy.

Even within the field of feminist studies, Haraway's thesis has been criticised as anti-feminist given that she is critical of the search for any essentialising unity. Countering what she takes to be the myth of commonality, she contends that there is nothing in terms of being 'female' which serves to inherently bind women — moreover, the hair-splitting search for 'a new essential unity' can only engender further conflict. She proffers affinity rather than identity, thereby denying a cohesive female experience. Underscoring this bold resolution, she signs off her *Manifesto* thus: 'I would rather be a cyborg than a goddess'.

***

Food for thought:

- Given our ever-growing reliance on technology, to what extent are we already, in some sense, cyborgs?
- Are we becoming ever more composite beings?
- Do we have (or did we ever have) an essential nature?
- To what extent does a being that is, as it were, 'non-essential' challenge the various dualisms posited by philosophy?
- Is the use of irony and/or playful contradiction ever justified in a serious philosophical text?
- Should we be wary of a philosophical text that is readily open to alternative interpretations?
- Is a dialectical synthesis, wherein all contradictions supposedly resolve themselves, a dangerous pipedream which we should reject?
- Is there nothing about being 'female' that naturally binds women?
- Does the appeal to a fundamental 'nature' or essence itself bind or constrict one?
- Should we appeal to a sense of affinity instead of identity?
- Would you rather be a cyborg or a goddess?

CHAPTER IV

T. E. Hulme: Schismatic Poetics

"I had been released from a nightmare which had long troubled my mind..."

Whilst apparently immersed in deep thought, the philosopher-poet T. E. Hulme (1883–1917), failed to hear the incoming artillery shell. As others ran for cover, he suffered a direct hit. His scant remains were buried in a military cemetery in Belgium. Yet despite his untimely death, Hulme was a significant, if somewhat offbeat philosopher whose work on aesthetics arguably shaped the trajectory of British literary modernism.

The son of a ceramic transfer manufacturer, Hulme was born on the 16 September 1883, in North Staffordshire. Showing no interest in taking over his father's business, Hulme attended St John's College, Cambridge. Although teetotal and a non-smoker, Hulme courted the company of so-called 'drunken rowdies' and was duly sent down from Cambridge for allegedly 'over-stepping the limits of traditional licence allowed by the authorities on Boat Race night'. His boisterous antics in a theatre resulted in the police being called and he was charged with being drunk and disorderly; Hulme denied being drunk but admitted to being 'excited'. As Hulme's uncle, Edward Hollinshead put it, 'my nephew, who is a very strong, tall young fellow instead of slipping half a crown into the hands of the policemen put up his back and bowled two of them over'. Hulme's family were both horrified and humiliated by his behaviour; for a while, his father refused to have anything to do with him. Hulme tried to bring up the subject of philosophy, pleading with his father to allow him to read the subject by way of a second chance. His father would have none of it, inquiring as to the use of such a frivolous subject? 'In North Staffordshire,' Hulme replied, 'no use at all.' Eventually, his father relented somewhat, and Hulme embarked on a study of botany and physics at University College, London, in October 1904; the course in some respects pandered to his father's aspirations for something more utilitarian. Living in London for the next two years, Hulme's studies did not progress well. However, he fed his appetite for philosophy by unofficially attending undergraduate lectures at Cambridge. His prodigious wanderings also negatively impacted his studies; he once spent three days walking home to Endon, sleeping rough in hedgerows and vacant barns. On other occasions, he walked to Bath and Oxford. Eventually, Hulme's academic moonlighting and aberrant lifestyle took its toll — he relinquished the gown and took passage on a cargo steamer to Montreal, Canada where he worked as a labourer on farms and lumber camps. When he returned to England aboard a cattle boat, there was no reconciliation with his family. After a brief interval studying French and German in Brussels, he returned to England once more and embarked on a private study of philosophy. This period of study produced a fragmented corpus of work that can be seen to harbour the seeds of the modernist aesthetic.

Hulme's thought was originally shaped by the work of the French philosopher, Henri Bergson (1859–1941), whom he met in 1907. Bergson heralded Hulme as a 'spirit of great worth' within the 'domain of philosophy'. In his turn, Hulme translated Bergson's *Introduction to Metaphysics*. For Hulme, Bergson's philosophy represented an escape from what he termed the 'prison house' of mechanistic determinism — a theory of being that holds future events to be as fixed and unalterable as past events. Within the parameters of such a theory of being, existence is preordained or wholly determined. For the early

Hulme, such fixity was an abomination. What he discovered in Bergson's intuitive thought was a liberation from all such overarching and delimiting notions. Building upon Bergson's philosophy, Hulme adhered to the idea that the whole of reality is shaped by an abiding plurality which he likened to an ashen chaos: 'In this ash-pit of cinders, certain ordered routes have been made, thus constituting whatever unity there may be — a kind of manufactured chess-board laid on a cinder-heap'. Yet this manufactured chessboard, impressed as it is upon the ashen chaos, has no veridical status; it represents the gossamer world of synthetic truths or symbolic categories. This fluid theory of being or ontology also accorded with Hulme's reading of Nietzsche. Echoing the German maestro, Hulme declared all to be in flux; a fluidity that washed aside objective truth and any attendant ethical certainty. In his notes, Hulme describes the emancipatory force of these ideas in what are almost revelatory terms: 'I felt the exhilaration that comes with the sudden change from a cramped and contracted to a free and expanded state [...]. I had been released from a nightmare which had long troubled my mind. If I compare my nightmare to imprisonment in a small cell, then the door of that cell was for the first time thrown open.'

In 1908, Hulme delivered a lecture before the members of the Poets' Club in London. Therein, he aligned his fluid concept of being with an aesthetic doctrine. According to Hulme's thesis, the ancients recognised and reacted against the abiding flux — they attempted to evade it through the construction of things of permanence. Such constructions, they hoped, would stand fast in the ever-present flux; a flux that generated ontological disquiet. 'Living in a dynamic world,' Hulme reasoned, 'they wished to create a static fixity where their souls might rest.' In accord with Aristotle, poetry was thus concerned with universal truths or archetypes. Such aesthetic universality led to a fixity of form and the founding of constraining rules of regular meter. Such rigidity of form was concordant with a fixed or static concept of the beyond. In short, the obsessive use of meter and regular syllabic form was the manifest product of an archaic approximation of an illusory beyond. He likened the use of such regular meter to cumbersome armour that serves to radically restrict the fluid movement of the avant-garde spirit. In its turn, this new and radical spirit manifests itself in a poetic form which has 'become definitely and finally introspective and deals with [the] expression and communication of momentary phases in the poet's mind'. Thus it was that Hulme called for the abandonment of any appeal to absolutism and any concomitant *ars perfecta* — this abandonment being couched in the name of an aesthetic that embraces the essential fluidity of modern being as understood by Bergson and Nietzsche. Through Hulme, such subjectivism acted as a catalyst for an aesthetic that was prevalent for much of the twentieth century. As his biographer, Robert Ferguson puts it, Hulme can be readily regarded as 'one of the half-dozen midwifes' to the Modernist aesthetic, influencing luminaries such as Ezra Pound and T. S. Eliot.

Yet despite this legacy, Hulme later disavowed such subjectivism in favour of an appeal to a form of neoclassical absolutism; in effect, he thus turned his former ideas on their head. Rejecting the teachings of Bergson and Nietzsche, he discovered in the work of the German phenomenologist, Edmund Husserl (1859–1938), a means by which to exhume an absolute from what he termed the 'cinder heap' of reality. In short, for the later Hulme, the flux harboured a residual absolute — the same absolute lauded in the formerly denigrated classical aesthetic. In an even more extreme change of tack, he also endorsed the philosophical objectivism he took to underlie the geometric aesthetic of the modernist sculptor Jacob Epstein.

It is believed that Hulme was carrying the only manuscript of his book on Epstein when he was killed in action.

Significantly, Hulme's bipartite thought can also be interpreted in ethical terms. His earlier radical subjectivism dovetailed with the philosophical egoism prevalent in certain British intellectual circles prior to the outbreak of the First World War. Within the terms of such egoism, what appear to be unassailable rights and duties are subordinated to the capricious will of the self-centred ego. For the likes of influential egoists such as Max Stirner, even love is a matter of self-centred utility: 'love rises in selfishness, flows in the bed of selfishness, and empties into selfishness again'. The later absolutism Hulme proffered fares little better in ethical terms, placing objective value above all else, including life itself. In 1916, Bertrand Russell (1872–1970) openly attacked Hulme's later ethic which countered his own pacifism. In Russell's opinion, Hulme was 'an evil man who could have created nothing but evil' had he survived the war.

Hulme did not survive the war, but his legacy has. Indeed, there is little doubt that the often capricious and bellicose Hulme sired a schismatic philosophy which served to radically alter aesthetic practice in the twentieth century. In 1924, the poet T. S. Eliot suggested that Hulme's philosophy signified 'a new attitude of mind' — that of the twentieth century.

***

Food for thought:

- Are future events as fixed and unalterable as past events, or is there an escape from the so-called 'prison house' of mechanistic determinism?
- Is reality shaped by a fluidity that washes aside objective truth and any attendant ethical certainty?

- Is all in flux and the 'truth' an illusion?
- From the position of subjective lived experience, reality is a fleeting series of images. Are such images the true subject matter of a poetry of 'life'?
- Should art and poetry *always* be governed by a freedom from extrinsic fetters?
- Is there perhaps artistic freedom within aesthetic constraints?
- Aristotle once suggested that poetry is more philosophical and more worthy of serious attention than history, given that poetry interrogates universal truths, whilst history's domain is particular facts. Can poetry be regarded as more truthful than history?
- Can art be construed as a means to the universal or underlying truth?
- Are aesthetic positions inescapably wedded to ethical concerns?
- How are we to judge thinkers that radically change their position?
- Are *ad hominem* arguments ever justifiable?
- To what extent might academia stifle radical thought?

CHAPTER V

Nicolas Malebranche: Causation and God

So thrilled was Malebranche by the ideas he encountered he had "violent palpitations of the heart".

So often dismissive of his contemporaries, the controversialist, Pierre Bayle, did more than just hold fire when it came to Nicolas Malebranche (1638–1715); instead, he heralded him as one of the greatest thinkers of his time. Indeed, within the Francophone world, Malebranche has long been extolled as a figure of central importance, not least in terms of his offbeat development of Cartesian philosophy. Until recently, within the Anglo-American tradition, things have been somewhat different. For example, in Russell's *History of Western Philosophy*, there are no more than three offhand references to Malebranche. However, recent translations have served to reignite interest in this often-unorthodox thinker.

Born in Paris in August 1638, the young Nicolas was by all accounts a frail child. Due in part to a painful malformation of the spine, he was educated at home; his pious mother, Catherine de Lauzon, provided watchful supervision. Later, he studied at the Collège de la Marche and subsequently the Sorbonne, becoming ever more dissatisfied with the ladles of Aristotelian thought served up as part of his Scholastic education. Having rejected a canonry at Notre-Dame de Paris, he entered the Oratory in 1660 — an order founded by Cardinal Bérulle, a theologian credited with encouraging Descartes' own philosophical speculations. In 1664, Malebranche was ordained.

Whilst ambling along the rue Saint Jacques in Paris, so the story goes, Malebranche stumbled upon an edition of Descartes' *Traité de l'homme* on a bookstall. His early biographer, Yves

André, recounts the immediate impact of Descartes' thought; so thrilled was Malebranche by the ideas he encountered, he had 'violent palpitations of the heart' which obliged him to stop reading and 'recover his breath'. What he discovered in the work of Descartes was an antidote to what he perceived to be the sterility of Aristotelian thought. In the wake of this discovery, Malebranche devoted the next ten years of his life to a study of Cartesian natural philosophy and mathematics; a study culminating in the publication of *De la recherche de la vérité* (*The Search After Truth*). Therein, he attempted to prove that the relationship between the human mind and God is 'natural, necessary, and absolutely indispensable'. This theocentric thread runs through two of his most famous doctrines: occasionalism and the vision in God.

Occasionalism is the doctrine that God is the sole causal agent; in this manner, all finite entities (including humans) lack true causal agency. In practice, Malebranche argued that when, for example, one stubs one's toe, the physical event is an 'occasion' for God to cause the appropriate mental state of pain. In reverse, a willed action such as walking or thinking of something is likewise an 'occasion' for God to cause one's legs to move or the relevant thoughts to flow before the mind. Within the broader context of the physical world, an axe blow is an 'occasion' for God to cleave wood. In all such instances, he argues, there are 'no forces, powers, or true causes in the material, sensible world'. Anticipating David Hume's causal scepticism, he concludes that 'one should not imagine that what precedes an effect is its true cause'.

Yet Malebranche was no theological reactionary. On the contrary, as offbeat or bizarre as it might at first appear, he saw his idea of causation as sitting perfectly well with the new mechanistic science of his age. As he argues, God's primary causal role does not negate mechanical considerations, for when God acts on bodies, his manner of interaction is always in accord with the laws of nature as set down in the original act of creation. In short then, scientific causal explanations still stand when it comes to investigating the natural world. In fact, Malebranche ridiculed any purely theocentric account: 'I grant that recourse to God as the universal cause should not be had when the explanation of a particular effect is sought'. In this manner, whilst deferring 'true' causation to God, Malebranche harmonised his seemingly dissonant occasionalism with natural science.

Although he praised what he termed Malebranche's 'fine reflections', Leibniz was critical of his use of God as the one true cause. Following Leibniz's mark, many modern critics have dismissed Malebranche's occasionalism as an act of ad hocism cobbled together in an attempt to resolve the problem of causal interaction in Cartesian dualism. Within the terms of Descartes' substance dualism, the un-extended immaterial mind and the extended physical body interact. Even without invoking the breach of the first law of thermodynamics, it is hard to fathom how such very different substances can interact. Princess Elisabeth of Bohemia pointed out this problem to Descartes in a deferential exchange of letters in 1643. Descartes' rather unconvincing rejoinders go some way to illustrating the gravity of the problem. However, Malebranche addresses the problem by denying any such causal interaction: 'it is God who is the true cause' he argued, and hence it is that 'bodies, minds, pure intelligences, all these can do nothing.'

And yet rather than being little more than an *ad hoc* response to the problem of causal interaction, Malebranche's solution issues, in part, from a subtle reading of Descartes' account of the relationship between God and the created world. Descartes argues that God conserves the self through a continuous act of creation. In this manner, God is a sustaining causal agent that creates the self anew, from moment to moment. Linking this continuous process of creation with the omnipresent causal agency of God, Malebranche reasons that God is the sustaining cause in all that one does. In this manner, he supposedly eliminates the problem of causal interaction whilst being true to core aspects of Cartesian thought. Setting aside the obvious theocentric bias, one might of course wonder why it is any less of a problem to posit an immaterial deity as a cause over and above an immaterial finite mind.

Malebranche's other core doctrine, the vision in God, dovetails with his occasionalism. Just as all human action is wholly dependent upon God, he argues that so too is all human cognition. That is to say, as knowers, we are cognitively dependent upon the workings of the divine understanding in much the same manner as bodies in motion are dependent upon the divine will. In line with Descartes' thinking, Malebranche regarded ideas, or immaterial representations before the mind, as centrally important in terms of human knowledge and perception. Yet at this juncture, Malebranche breaks ranks with Cartesian thought by offering a subtly different account. For Descartes, ideas are essentially mental entities. Malebranche ventures that, on the contrary, all ideas exist within God alone and are therefore independent of finite minds. In accord with this reasoning, Malebranche tenders a radical conclusion: 'on this view, not only could we see nothing but what He wills that we see, but we could see nothing but what He makes us see.' In short, we see all things in God — *nous voyons toutes choses en Dieu*.

By the mid-1680s, many considered Malebranche to be the most significant, albeit somewhat offbeat advocate of the Cartesian philosophy. But more than this, he had a direct, if largely unsung, influence on other key philosophical developments. His work on causation and vision was instrumental in the development of early eighteenth-century idealism for example. In addition, there is an argument to be made that Hume owed an intellectual debt to Malebranche, drawing upon his negative arguments when formulating his own scepticism with regard to genuine causal connections and the knowability of the self. In terms of the latter argument, it seems that Malebranche's account of the unknowability of the self is remarkedly similar to Hume's famous 'Personal Identity' section in his *Treatise on Human Nature* — as Malebranche argues, 'I am unable to discover the relations of the modifications which affect my soul. By entering into myself (*"en me tournant vers moi-même"*) I cannot discover any of my faculties or capacities. My inner self reveals only that I am, that I think, that I desire, that I feel, that I suffer, etc.; but it does not reveal to me what I am, the nature of my feelings, of my passions, of my pain, nor the relations of all these to one another, because having no idea of my soul, not beholding its archetype in God, I am not able to discover either what it is or the modes of which it is capable.' If the debate surrounding influence or confluence is open regarding Hume, a concrete connection can be seen in the case of Leibniz whom Malebranche met in Paris; thereafter the two philosophers struck up a productive correspondence between 1675 and 1712. At least in part, Leibniz's famous system of pre-established harmony can be construed as a novel alternative to Malebranche's occasionalism. For Leibniz, rather than God interceding as the one and only true causal agency, seeming interaction can be accounted for by God having, in advance, as it were, harmonised what appear to be causes and effects — such harmony circumventing the problem of causal interaction. Moreover, Leibniz's theodicy is arguably indebted to Malebranche's own attempt to reconcile God's beneficence with the existence of evil. In his *Essais de Théodicée*, Leibniz suggested that his theodicy was similar to Malebranche's in key respects, concluding that Malebranche's position could be reduced to his own. Malebranche underscored this connection when he wrote, 'I am persuaded as you are ... that God gave to creatures all the good that he can give them' and thus 'his work is the most perfect that it can be'.

This said, Malebranche also suffered at the hands of some vocal detractors, not least the Cartesian partisan, Antoine Arnauld. With the publication of Malebranche's *Traité de la Nature et de la Grace* (1680), Arnauld launched a detailed critique; the first salvo in a protracted and often bitter theological dispute which culminated in Arnauld and his supporters having some of Malebranche's key works placed on the Roman Catholic *Index Librorum Prohibitorum*. Later critics included Schopenhauer, who suggested that Malebranche's vision in God was tantamount 'to explaining something unknown by something even more unknown'. Taking the vision in God and occasionalism together, Schopenhauer proclaimed that what the combined theories boiled down to was essentially 'the pantheism of Spinoza who appears to have learnt more from Malebranche than from Descartes'. Although he didn't make his case as explicit, Leibniz also regarded occasionalism as tending towards the notion that God is the only true substance. Locke echoed this censure, adding that Malebranche's doctrine of seeing all things in God was one step away from an out-and-out denial of material objects. Having read Malebranche, the likes of George Berkeley and Arthur Collier were happy to take this final step into immaterialism.

Arguably, the aforesaid censure speaks volumes in terms of the tacit impact of Malebranche's radical philosophy. Whilst often regarded as something of a peripheral figure, Malebranche's contribution to the development of Western philosophy cannot be denied. As the Malebranche scholar, Steven Nadler, claims, it is only now that the radical Cartesian is 'finding his rightful place in the pantheon of early modern thinkers'.

***

Food for thought:

- Are you essentially two substances: a material body and an immaterial mind/soul?
- Or are you matter in motion and everything about you is, at least in theory, explainable by physics?
- Are you an immaterial mind or soul and the physical body is an illusion?
- Supposing you are composed of two substances, mind and body, how do these very different substances interact?
- Consider how it would be possible for an immaterial cog to interact or mesh with a material cog. If we extrapolate from this example, how can the immaterial mind animate the material body? How can a thought (rather than a brain process) cause the body to move or act?
- More broadly, what causes things to happen in the universe?
- Do your desires and your will cause things to happen in the world?
- If we posit the idea of an omnipotent god, what would be the causal nature of such a deity? What would such a god cause to happen in the universe?
- Could it be that such a god is the only causal agent in the universe? Are my thoughts, desires, etc mediated by God in terms of their effects?
- When faced with a deeply problematic issue in philosophy, is the use of God as an 'antidote' (the 'God of the gaps') always intellectually suspect?
- If God is omniscient, do all our finite ideas in some sense subsist in the divine mind?
- When we self-reflect or apperceive, do we ever encounter the self?

CHAPTER VI

Paul Rée: The Myth of Free Will

"Responsibility is a chimera which stalks the conscience of those who are not bold enough to apply the deterministic laws of nature to themselves..."

In 1878, Nietzsche wrote a letter to Paul Rée (1849–1901) in which he declared: 'All my friends are now agreed that my book [*Human, All-Too-Human*] comes from and is written by you: so I congratulate you on this new authorship ... Long live Réealism and my good friend!' Although this friendship was not to last, many commentators agree that Rée had a profound, if temporary, influence on both Nietzsche's thought and his method of philosophical expression. Arguably, this broad consensus gives weight to the idea that Rée helped to shape the course of modern continental philosophy, albeit from the intellectual sidelines.

However, Rée was a radical philosopher in his own right. He was a hard-nosed empiricist who rejected appeals to metaphysics, religion and the notion of free will. Via an appeal to Darwin's theory of natural selection, he also repudiated *a priori* moral principles, going as far as to proclaim that we should abandon the notion of moral responsibility not merely in theory, but in practice as well. As he put it, 'someone who has recognized the nonfreedom of the will no longer holds anyone responsible'.

Paul Ludwig Carl Heinrich Rée was born in Bartelshagen, a village in Pomerania close to the Baltic coast. His parents were both from assimilated Jewish families, a lineage that was later exploited by the anti-Semitic Wagnerian circle as they tried to distance themselves from Nietzsche. In 1869, Rée embarked on a study of philosophy and law at the University of Leipzig. Following an interval in which he fought in the Franco-Prussian war, he devoted himself to the study of philosophy at the University of Halle; his doctoral dissertation interrogated the notion of nobility within the context of Aristotelian ethics.

Rée and Nietzsche first met in Basel in the summer of 1873. As their friendship developed, Nietzsche began to laud Rée, likening him to a skilful marksman adept at hitting the bullseye of human nature time and again. In 1882, Rée introduced Nietzsche to the young Russian bohemian, Lou Salomé (later Lou Andreas-Salomé). Within days of meeting, the three thinkers were travelling together in Italy. In Lucerne they posed for the now infamous photograph in which Nietzsche and Rée appear tethered to a cart whilst Lou Salomé stoops behind them wielding a whip. Rée strongly objected to the pose, but Nietzsche insisted. Regretfully, it is within this context that Rée is often remembered today.

Yet Rée's thought warrants serious academic attention, especially when set within the framework of the free will and determinism debate. According to Rée, every act of the will is preceded by what he terms a 'sufficient cause'. As he points out, without such a cause the act of willing cannot itself occur. Drawing out this thread of reason, Rée stipulates that if the sufficient cause is present, the act of willing must occur *sub specie necessitatis* (under the aspect of necessity). The conclusion is that the notion of free will entails a departure from the causal laws which govern the universe. As he puts it, each act of willing would be an absolute beginning or first cause of and by itself. For Rée this is patent nonsense, and hence he is able to conclude that free will is a manifest illusion. Rée accounts for the power of this ever-present illusion by suggesting that we do not perceive the causes by which our choices and desires are determined, and hence it is that we labour under the false impression that our volition is free from causal necessity. Focusing on the notion of pity, he gives voice to this micro-macro dialectic thus: 'Suppose, for example, that I am stirred by a feeling of pity at this moment. To what causes is it to be attributed? Let us go back as far as possible. An infinite amount of time has elapsed up to this moment. Time was never empty; objects have filled all eternity. These objects ... have continually undergone change. All these changes were governed by the law of causality; not one of them took place without a sufficient cause. [...] We need not consider what else may have characterised these changes. Only their formal aspect, only this one point is of concern to us: no change occurred without a [deterministic] cause.' Numerous other philosophers have drawn similar conclusions. Yet what is radical about Rée is his uncompromising nerve when it comes to drawing out the logical consequences of this deterministic picture of the self. As he makes plain, moral responsibility is based on the error of supposing that humans possess free will — when 'we have understood the necessity of all human actions, we no longer hold anyone responsible'.

Rée concedes that as with the one-time believer who has managed to shake off the fetters of religion, the yoke of moral responsibility might still weigh heavy in the mind like an absent God: 'is it really possible to shake off feelings of guilt so easily? Do they disappear, like a spook, when the magic word effect is pronounced?' To offset this atavism, Rée suggests that whenever someone involuntarily wants to ascribe blame or praise to an action, they should ascend to what he terms the 'point of view of eternity and necessity'. From such an intellectual vantage point, from a macro-cosmic perspective, the 'instinctual association between the action and the judgement will be severed, if not for the first time, then perhaps for the thousandth'. With reference to Sophocles, Simon Critchley argues that in what appears to be our 'free, volitional action there is an experience of being acted upon by a curse'. As Oedipus puts it, 'all the events that have thrust themselves upon me [...] The Gods so willed it — doubtless an ancient grudge / Against our house'. Rée replaces the Theban curse with the cold indifference of a universal causality that serves to negate all freedom and responsibility.

Moreover, Critchley has recently argued that many of the characters portrayed in Greek tragedies occupy a space within which they are neither free nor causally determined. Ostensibly, they dwell in a performative locus set 'between freedom and necessity, where both are present, deeply interdependent, yet quite distinct'. As he argues, it is perhaps pre-Platonic Greek drama which can harbour the incongruities of lived experience shaped by the play of such opposed forces. By virtue of this play of opposites, such drama can posit (but not answer) the intractable and multivalent Aeschylean question: *ti draso*? ('What should I do?') — a question which is arguably 'not the beginning of an experience of rational argumentation, but reason's terminus'.

Before reaching this terminus, numerous philosophical attempts have been made to mix the oil and water of freedom and necessity. Yet despite the labours of such luminaries as Hobbes and Hume, this mix appears to be stubbornly immiscible when stirred by the logic of hard-nosed empirical philosophy. Could it be the case that rather than being an awakening to freedom and moral responsibility, *ti draso*? can be reconfigured as a traumatic moment wherein one becomes conscious of the seeming tragedy of necessity and the attendant vacuity of all ethical deliberation? In other words, given the play of universal necessity, must the question, 'What should I do?' always be asked with a mind to the redundancy of real choice and ultimate responsibility? Rendering *libertas* a myth, the work of Rée would have it so.

Rée's position could not be further removed from that of later existential thinkers such as Sartre. For Sartre, determinism is false: 'there is no determinism — man [sic] is free, man is freedom'. In stark contrast to Rée, such liberty entails total responsibility. As Sartre puts it, the first principle of existentialism 'is that it puts every man [sic] in possession of himself as he is, and places the entire responsibility for his existence squarely upon his own shoulders'. In Rée's uncompromising estimation, such responsibility is a chimera which stalks the conscience of those who are not bold enough to apply the deterministic laws of nature to themselves.

At the turn of the century, Rée spent a year retracing his former travels with Lou Salomé. He stayed in Celerina in Switzerland for over a year; it was one of the last places he and Lou Salomé had visited during their travels together. Walking above the Charnadüre Gorge near Celerina, Rée apparently slipped and then fell to his death. He had once argued that the decision to kill oneself arises from an excess of rationality. Although the Swiss authorities returned a verdict of accidental death, there has been much speculation as to the true nature of Rée's tragic end — by the light of his own offbeat logic, an end set whilst 'unbegotten, unconceived' (Sophocles).

***

Food for thought:

- What is the nature of freedom?
- Are we free, and if so, in what sense?
- Is liberty synonymous with freedom?
- What would be the necessary conditions of so-called free will?
- If science is underpinned by the notions of universal causation and causal necessity, does this negate any sense of free will?

- If a chain of cause and effect can be traced back to the beginning of the universe, does this entail that our lives, our thoughts and our willed actions are nothing but determined facets of an unfolding cosmos?
- If determinism is true, does this render all ethical responsibility redundant?
- Is it possible to be both free and determined? Can we mix the metaphoric oil and water of freedom and necessity?
- Does the question, 'What should I do?' entail profound freedom and responsibility?
- Is freedom the very foundation of what it is to be human?
- Even if determinism is true, can one live by such a truth? Can theory lead to praxis?

CHAPTER VII

Clive Bell: The Value of Art

It is "useless to go into a picture gallery in search of expression;
you must go in search of significant form".

The British philosopher and art critic, Clive Bell (1881–1964), was a prominent proponent of the formalist approach to aesthetics. In this specific sense, he advocated and significantly developed an aesthetic ethos stemming back to the work of Kant. According to Kant, what we value in a work of art is its formal qualities. In *Art* (1914), Bell outlined his own offbeat take on this approach to aesthetics — an approach that served to rationalise emergent modernist practices as exemplified in the work of Post-Impressionists such as Paul Cézanne (1839–1906).

Clive Bell was born in East Shefford, Berkshire. He was the son of Hannah Taylor Cory and William Heward Bell, the latter being a wealthy industrialist. Whilst studying at Trinity College, Cambridge, Bell met and befriended a number of the later leading lights in the Bloomsbury Group. In 1907, he married the artist Vanessa Stephen, the sister of the eminent modernist writer, Virginia Woolf. Both husband and wife became prominent figures in the Bloomsbury circle and there is little doubt that Bell's association with this group of leading English intellectuals significantly shaped his radical aesthetic vision. In 1910, Bell also met the prominent art critic and painter, Roger Fry. The ensuing friendship further contributed to the development of Bell's own particular brand of formalism. Moreover, the influential American modernist writer and art collector, Gertrude Stein, took Bell to Picasso's studio in

Montparnasse in 1911; by all accounts, the painter and the critic struck up an enduring friendship.

Whilst championing the avant-garde movement, Bell set himself the task of challenging the traditional assumption that the value of visual art is in some way located in its representative or mimetic function. Indeed, according to Bell's argument, the representative element in a work of art is largely irrelevant in terms of our appreciation of it as a significant cultural artefact. To appreciate a work of art, 'we need bring nothing with us but a sense of form and colour' he argued. This seemingly hard-nosed formalism harbours one concession; as Bell grants, pictures that would be 'insignificant' if we saw them as two-dimensional patterns are sometimes profoundly moving because, in point of fact, we perceive them as three-dimensional related planes. This admission is Bell's only concession to the mimetic mode — a mode famously lambasted by Plato in *The Republic* as sitting at 'third remove from the throne of truth' (see: 10.597e).

Issuing out of this censure was Bell's central contribution to the philosophy of art, namely, his innovative theory of significant form. According to Bell, artists are in the business of combining lines and colours in such a way as to aesthetically move the sensitive observer. Significant form is the artistic arrangement of such lines and colours; an arrangement that serves to provoke what Bell terms an aesthetic emotion. Yet in Bell's estimation, not all form is significant. Indeed, he was scathing with regard to popular representative paintings such as William Powell Frith's *The Railway Station* (1862) which he deemed to be nothing more than an 'interesting and amusing document'. Although such paintings contain formal elements, they lack what Bell held to be the 'one quality common to all works of visual art' — in short, significant form. Besides, he argued, 'with the perfection of photographic processes and [...] cinematography, pictures of this sort are becoming otiose.'

Unlike the Oxford philosopher, R. G. Collingwood (1889–1943), and the Italian philosopher, Benedetto Croce (1866–1952), Bell distanced himself from the idea that 'art proper' is valuable in terms relating to the expression of the emotions. According to Collingwood, the value of art for both the artist and the viewer resides in its capacity to elucidate and individuate the emotions: 'The characteristic mark of expression proper is lucidity or intelligibility; a person who expresses something thereby becomes conscious of what it is that he [sic] is expressing, and enables others to be conscious of it in himself and in them'.

Bell countered such aesthetic idealism by suggesting that it is 'useless to go into a picture gallery in search of expression; you must go in search of significant form'. However, this is not to say that the emotions play no part in the creative process itself. On the contrary, Bell argues that 'true artists' are able to experience objects as pure form and it is this experience of objects devoid of all function and attendant associations that generates what he terms an inspired emotion. It is this profound emotion that functions as a catalyst for the creation of true and significant art. This said, Bell is adamant that the value of such art resides exclusively in its formal qualities rather than in any notion of expressive modality.

In a somewhat speculative section of *Art* entitled 'The Metaphysical Hypothesis', Bell also appears to echo Schopenhauer when he proffers the idea that significant form constitutes a vehicle by which the sensitive spectator can glimpse the structures of what he terms 'essential reality' — be it construed as the 'God in everything', the 'universal in the particular', or an 'all-pervading rhythm'. In other words, Bell suggests that significant form acts as an aperture through which to apprehend 'that which lies behind the appearance of all things — that which gives all things their individual significance, the thing in itself'. Accepting the speculative nature of his metaphysical theory, he asks, are 'we to swallow it whole' or 'accept a part of it'; or should we 'reject it altogether?' Whilst maintaining the 'rightness' of his broader aesthetic hypothesis, he concedes that, 'each must decide for himself [sic]'. Roger Fry decided not to plunge headlong into the depths of such mysticism: 'On the edge of that gulf I must stop'. On the other hand, the evaluation of D. H. Lawrence was more forthright; he concluded that, far from being an aperture unto the metaphysical 'beyond', significant form 'is a bogy which doesn't exist' — or more colourfully, it is little more than 'a form of masturbation, an attempt to make the body react to some cerebral formula'.

Setting aside such heated debate for a moment, the question now arises as to how one is supposed to be aware of significant form. Like many other members of the Bloomsbury Group, Bell was profoundly influenced by the work of the Cambridge philosopher G. E. Moore. According to Moore, ethical terms such as 'good' are indefinable; one is aware of that which is good via an act of intuition. Analogously, Bell put forward the idea that the sensitive observer of a work of art is aware of significant form by way of a comparable act of intuitive cognisance. Wielding this brand of aesthetic intuitionism, Bell came to the somewhat elitist conclusion that those who remain unmoved whilst in the presence of such form are like 'deaf men at a concert'. It would appear that Bell's logic dictates that good art is the preserve of a sensitive and cultured minority. As Nigel Warburton aptly puts it, Bell's aesthetic seems to constitute 'little more than the elevation of an individual's taste into an objective ideal'. In an earlier riposte, D. H. Lawrence also chided the Bloomsbury intellectuals for proffering an aesthetic experience, 'granted only to the chosen few, the elect', with critics such as Bell being the self-appointed 'arch-elect'.

Aside from such charges of elitism, Bell's theory is also perhaps guilty of propagating a rather dubious essentialism.

According to Bell, all works of visual art must have something in common; as he asserts, there must be 'some one quality without which a work of art cannot exist' — otherwise, he concludes, when we speak of works of art we gibber. However, set within the terms of Wittgenstein's notion of family resemblances, 'good art' can be meaningfully defined within a complex network of overlapping features. To employ Wittgenstein's metaphor, there is perhaps no single significant thread holding together our conception of what good art is. If this is the case, contrary to Bell's argument, it is not significant form which is a common denominator in art as diverse as Giotto's frescoes at Padua and a Persian bowl. Rather, our notion of significant art can be construed as a conceptual amalgamation, the strength of which, to quote Wittgenstein, 'does not reside in the fact that some one fibre runs through its whole length, but in the overlapping of many fibres'. Within these terms, the 'many' negates the singularity of any appeal to significant form.

Moreover, Bell's focus on the universality of formal qualities, seemingly 'independent of time and place', decontextualises art. As he argues, so-called great art 'remains stable and unobscured' — this being the case because 'its kingdom is not of this world'. And yet surely much of the value of a painting such as Picasso's *Guernica* (1937) resides within the context of the image, not merely within its formal qualities, as striking, and indeed as significant, as these might be. Arguably, such a painting would lose its power and significance if isolated from its subject matter, the destruction of the Basque town of Guernica during the Spanish Civil War. It is to be noted that in 1937, Bell's son, Julian, enlisted as an ambulance driver in the Spanish conflict; shortly afterwards, he died as a result of injuries sustained at the Battle of Brunete. Two months beforehand, in May 1937, Picasso had shown Bell's wife, Vanessa, the almost completed *Guernica*, deliberating with her the merits and demerits of introducing more colour to the now famous monochromatic canvas. Bell himself maintained a friendship with Picasso that lasted some fifty years, but given the death of their son in Spain, it is to be doubted whether either Vanessa or Clive could have ever contemplated a work such as *Guernica* within the strict limits of formal exaltation.

Setting aside this *argumentum ad hominem*, one of the criticisms often levelled against Bell's argument for significant form is that it is circular. The English painter and critic, Roger Fry, was one of the first to highlight the possible fallacy of circularity at play in Bell's work. Thomas M. McLaughlin précises thus: 'Bell's critics usually formulate his circular thinking in this way: he begins his analysis by asserting the existence of a purely aesthetic emotion, and then argues that all art must possess some quality to which this emotion responds, that is, significant form, which he then defines as form capable of stirring aesthetic emotion'. McLaughlin concedes that this sketch is rather reductive and does not, as such, represent the subtlety of Bell's reasoning. Indeed, even if construed as circular, there is arguably a sense in which Bell's position is not *viciously* circular and thus remains 'informative'. As Warburton puts it, defenders of Bell would argue that his theory 'is not viciously circular as it sheds light on why some people are better critics than others, namely because they have a better ability to detect significant form'. But have we not at this juncture turned full circle and returned to our earlier charge; namely that Bell is proffering a dubious form of intuitionism issuing from the elitist and somewhat insular mindset of the Bloomsbury clique?

Yet despite these criticisms, Bell's offbeat take on art constitutes a significant intervention in the field of modern aesthetics. Indeed, Bell's denigration of representation in the name of formal significance provided the developing modernist movement with a philosophical rationale. Furthermore, as the critic S. P. Rosenbaum has suggested, Bell's *Art* can be regarded as one of the first Bloomsbury manifestos ranking alongside *The Economic Consequences of the Peace* by Keynes as a Bloomsbury polemic. Thus, for all its faults, the central importance of Bell's radical aesthetic cannot be so easily dismissed with assertions that it is tautological, over-simplistic, or aesthetically chimerical. In addition, more recently, researchers such as Semir Zeki have made plausible, if tentative, connections between significant form and objectively quantifiable activity in the mOFC or medial orbito-frontal cortex, thereby correlating neurobiological activity with Bell's rather abstract notion of 'unknown and mysterious' laws. Could it thus be that significant form can be mapped onto the neurobiological constitution of all human beings? Would such neural-receptivity render Bell's decontextualisation of art justified, and, by the same token, underscore his appeal to a formal aesthetic essence? Whatever the answer to these questions might turn out to be, Bell's aesthetic is still proving to be fertile ground for ongoing aesthetic deliberation.

***

Food for thought:

- What is it about works of art that we value?
- Does the value of a work of art reside in our emotional response to it? Is art of value because it stirs the emotions in some sense?
- Plato argued that because art stirs the emotions it is potentially corruptive, leading one away from the path of clear, rational thought. Is art anti-philosophical in this sense?
- Does *good* art have the capacity to stimulate feelings of ecstasy — a feeling of escapism or *ek-stasis* (being outside of one's self or one's 'stance')? Can one lose oneself in

art and, if so, what are the merits and demerits of this possibility?

- Is it not just our emotional response which is of value, but the sense in which the artwork is an expression of the artist's emotions? Are works of art literally expressive? Do we value art because it stimulates vicarious pleasures, pains, joys, etc?
- Or, as Bell argued, is it useless to go into a gallery in search of expression?
- Does the value of art reside in its formal qualities: the way in which the paint has been applied to the canvas, for example, the harmony or dissonance of the composition etc?
- The Greek term *kalon* means aesthetically beautiful. Do we value art in terms of its purely aesthetic qualities rather than its emotive modality? Or are these two facets inextricably linked?
- Is some art 'significant' because of its formal qualities?
- If so, what is the nature of this so-called 'significant form'? How are we aware of this quality? Are we aware of it via a form of aesthetic intuition or does such a suggestion harbour a dubious elitism?
- Is there an essence to art?
- Contrary to Plato, is there a possibility that art can open up the *beyond*, however that might be construed? In other words, could significant art stimulate metaphysical insight?

CHAPTER VIII

Princess Elisabeth of Bohemia: Mind and Motion

"Tell me how the human soul can determine the movement of the body?"

Princess Elisabeth of the Palatinate, also known as Princess Elisabeth of Bohemia, was born on 26 December 1618 in Heidelberg Castle. She was the eldest daughter of Elisabeth Stuart, whose father was James VI of Scotland and I of England and Ireland. Elisabeth's father was Fredrick V, Elector of Palatine and, briefly, King of Bohemia. When Fredrick lost his throne, Elisabeth's family went into exile in The Hague. Educated at the Prinsenhof in Leiden, Elisabeth was tutored in languages including Greek, Latin, German, French and English. Her broader education also seems to have included instruction in the sciences, politics, jurisprudence, mathematics and logic, as well as philosophy; professors at the University of Leiden supplementing her training. Indeed, such was her intellectual prowess, Elisabeth's siblings referred to her as *La Grecque* ('The Greek').

Elisabeth met Descartes in The Hague and visited him at his residence in Endegeest, near Leiden. Having read the *Meditations*, she began a seven-year correspondence with the philosopher which lasted until his death in 1650. Although she did not write systematic works of philosophy herself, what marks Elisabeth out as a philosopher of distinction is the manner in which she applied a deferential blade to Cartesian philosophy. At the very inception of so-called modern philosophy, Elisabeth challenged the burgeoning orthodoxy of interactionist substance dualism; her incisive lunges being poorly parried by the French master.

According to Descartes, the mind and the body are two separate ontological substances. The body, he argued, is divisible, whilst the mind is not. As he puts it in his *Sixth Meditation*, the mind appears to be one 'single and complete thing', whilst the body is divisible in the sense that one's foot or arm can be separated from the rest of one's body. Given this division and the conceivability of separation, he concludes that the mind or soul is entirely different from the material body. This conclusion dovetailed with his defence of Catholicism and appeared, on the face of it, highly intuitive. Indeed, one's body appears to move in accord with willed desires. In this way, so it seems, the mind and body causally interact with one another. One could of course challenge the veracity of substance dualism from a physicalist perspective; perhaps the so-called mind is merely an illusion, a 'ghost in the machine' as Gilbert Ryle was to later put it. But setting aside such external criticisms, Descartes' account appears to be internally flawed as Princess Elisabeth pointed out in her point-by-point critique.

Having drawn a distinction between the mind and body, Descartes appears entirely untroubled as to the problem of causal interaction. And yet how are two utterly distinct substances supposed to interact with one another? If one were to replace an iron cog in a clock with an immaterial substitute, would not the mechanism fail to function? Deriding such objections, Descartes responded thus: 'The whole problem contained in such questions arises simply from a supposition that is false and cannot in any way be proved, namely that, if the soul and the body are two substances whose nature is different, this prevents them from being able to act on each other'. Objects having different natures does not preclude their interaction; the phrase, 'the sound of leather on willow' illustrates the point well enough perhaps. Nevertheless, although leather and willow might be said to have different natures, they are, ontologically speaking, composed of the same-self substance; that is to say, they are both physical and thereby subject to physical causal laws. But in the case of the mind and the body, we are dealing with two entirely different substances; as in the earlier clock example, it is hard to see how such substances could *ever* interact. Likewise, if we consider spatial relationships, physical objects such as the body are in space whilst the mind, if it exists as a separate entity, is not in space. If the two are to interact, that which is in space and that which is not in space must act upon one another. In short, the soul or mind must, as it were, make contact with the body and vice versa, seemingly *per impossibile*.

Elisabeth takes Descartes to task on exactly this issue. Her May 1643 deconstruction of his position is worth quoting at length: 'Tell me how the human soul can determine the movement of the animal spirits in the body so as to perform voluntary acts — being as it is merely a conscious substance. For the determination of the movement seems always to come about from the moving body's being propelled — to depend on the kind of impulse it gets from what it sets in motion, or again, on the nature and shape of this latter thing's surface. Now the first two conditions involve contact, and the third involves that the impelling thing has extension; but you utterly exclude extension from your notion of soul, and contact seems to me incompatible with a thing's being immaterial'.

When Elisabeth refers to the 'animal spirits' she is referring to the *spiritus animalis* theory as propagated by Galen. Prior to the electrochemical understanding of the nervous system in the eighteenth century, it was believed that the muscles were animated (*anima*) by the 'animal spirits' which were construed as fine streams of air (*spiritus*). If we substitute *spiritus animalis* for signals within nerve fibres, we can see that, in the first instance, Elisabeth is questioning how the immaterial soul or mind (*res cogitans*) can interact with the physiological mechanics of the human body (*res extensa*). To unpack her logic a little further, she is maintaining that physical objects or 'bodies' (i) act upon one another and (ii) are likewise acted upon. Additionally, the surface of physical objects has a specific quality or shape which enables movement (iii). The first two conditions involve contact whilst the third requires extension. However, as Elisabeth makes plain, Descartes excludes extension from his notion of the soul or *res cogitans*, and contact appears to be wholly incompatible with a substance being immaterial. Consequently, how can the human soul determine the movement of the animal spirits?

In reply, Descartes argued that Elisabeth's outline of how things are propelled or moved was deficient. He cites the example of an object falling, its movement being accountable in terms of its weight. But weight, as he points out, does not 'push' the falling object; rather, it is a property of the object *per se*. In this sense, weight is dependent upon gravity and mass; gravity being a force of attraction which operates without 'contact' between objects. We can concede this point, but does it refute Elisabeth's criticism? It seems not, for we can extrapolate from the given instance of pushing to physical force in a more generalised sense. If we do this, the question still stands as to how the mind, which has no physical force, can possibly affect the body? As we saw earlier, the mind is said to be aspatial, and yet cause and effect, as generally conceived, involves spatial relations. One might thus be forgiven for concluding that Descartes is simply playing the philosophical pedant in the face of Elisabeth's polemic.

Writing on 1 July 1643, Elisabeth accepts that self-reflection reveals that the mind does indeed cause the body to move; yet the problem still remains as to how this is possible. Following this logic through, she floats the idea that perhaps the soul has properties that are unknown, an idea that might very well, as she points out, overturn the Cartesian idea that the soul is not extended. Yet a subtler reading of Descartes reveals that he is perhaps arguing that extension is not the *principal* epistemic attribute of the *res cogitans*. Indeed, as he put it, thought can be both extended and divisible in terms of duration, given that duration can itself be subdivided into parts. However, he clarifies, thought is not 'extended and divisible with respect to its nature, since it remains unextended'. If the mind remains unextended in its very nature, the problem of interaction remains. Descartes appears to echo Elisabeth's reservations in this regard when he grants: 'what belongs to the union of the soul and the body is known only obscurely by the intellect alone or even by the intellect aided by the imagination, but it is known very clearly by the senses'. In light of Elisabeth's criticism, to conceive of such causal union appears to lead to conceptual absurdity as Descartes appears to concede: 'It does not seem to me' he admits, 'that the human mind is capable of forming a very distinct conception of both the distinction between the soul and the body and their union; for to do this it is necessary to conceive them as a single thing and at the same time to conceive them as two things; and this is absurd.' Even Descartes' claim that the pineal gland acts as an interface between the mind and body does not redress Elisabeth's criticism — the postulated 'faces' must come into contact, which Elisabeth dismisses in the case of the interaction between mind and body. Given her criticisms, did Elisabeth advocate a form of materialism? As she accepts, 'it would be easier for me to concede matter and extension to the soul than to concede the capacity to move a body and be moved by it to an immaterial thing'. Yet despite this apparent concession to incipient materialism, she appears to have adhered to a form of dualism, albeit naturalistic in nature — this being the idea that the soul is conscious as well as extended, but in a manner precluding a full-blown descent into reductive materialism.

Through her erudite exchanges with Descartes, we thus gain an insight into an exceptional mind. She was an offbeat thinker who was willing and well-able to critically challenge a philosophical luminary of her day. But more than this, Elisabeth was no passive interlocutor or mere 'handmaiden' to the master philosopher. Instead, she forged her own distinctive metaphysical position which is still today the subject of partisan debate in academic circles. For his part, Descartes appears to have relished the intellectual cut-and-thrust; indeed, he dedicated his *Principia Philosophiae* (1644) to Elisabeth highlighting her steadfast acuity: 'only you understand perfectly all the treatises I have so far published up to this time. For to most others, even to the most gifted and learned, my works seem very obscure'.

In 1660, Elisabeth entered Herford Abbey in the Duchy of Saxony; in 1667 she became abbess and served in that capacity until her death, after a long illness, in 1680. Embracing fringe sects such as the Labadists and Quakers, tolerance seems to have been a feature of her stewardship at the Lutheran institution. 'My house and my heart shall be always open to those that love him [God]' she proclaimed. Contrary to Platonic teaching, she had once argued that philosophy and practical governance were to be regarded as exclusive pursuits. Her years as the Princess-Abbess at Herford *Frauenstift* seem to belie this claim. On her headstone, Elisabeth is eulogised in the following epitaph: 'Most Serene Princess and Abbess of Herford, born of Palatine Electors and Kings of Great Britain, unconquered and in all fortune full of constancy and fortitude, singularly capable and prudent in affairs and of an erudition worthy of wonder, celebrated beyond the condition of her sex, friend of learned men and of princes.'

***

Food for thought:

- How does something being conceivable relate to *that* something being possible?

- Can something in space act upon that which is not in space?
- You can will your hand to move: does this not prove that the mind and body interact?
- Does a radically different ontological constitution preclude the possibility of causal interaction?
- To what extent might a particular religious perspective impact one's view of the mind and body debate?
- Is the mind or soul merely an illusion — a 'ghost in the machine' as it were?
- Does modern neuroscience show substance dualism to be an anachronism?
- Are the mind and the body (the brain) the same type of thing seen in a different way? Could we ontologically reduce one to the other without loss of meaning?
- Is the mind/body problem merely a linguistic illusion based on a conceptual misunderstanding? Is it a fallacy of reasoning to ask how the mind and the body (the mental and the biological) interact? Are we attempting to describe one of the two terms in the vocabulary of the other and hence engaging in a contextual error? In other words, when we attempt to posit mental states in causal relation to brain states are we simply wielding mutually exclusive vocabularies; are we thus committing a so-called 'category mistake'? In short, is the mind/body problem linguistic or ontological at root?
- Are philosophy and practical governance (or politics) mutually exclusive pursuits? Does too much theory lead to real-world inertia? Or should governance, in accord with Plato, be based upon philosophical insight?

CHAPTER IX

Emmanuel Levinas: Ethics and Otherness

"Western philosophy has most often been an ontology: a reduction of the other to the same."

Despite being offbeat in both terms of content and style, the ethical philosophy of Emmanuel Levinas (1906–1995) has been hugely influential. This accolade is justified even though his work is devoid of what might be termed traditional ethical discourse. According to the often-multifaceted arguments of the naturalised French philosopher, such discourse presupposes what can be construed as a profound ethical encounter that gives rise to one's sense of subjective being. Figuratively, rather than playing to the beat of normative ethical debate, Levinas gestures towards a discourse which subverts such debate. In short, in order to debate at all, one is *always already* the product of an ethical encounter.

Levinas was born in Kovno, Lithuania, in January 1906. Having completed his secondary education in Ukraine, he studied philosophy in conjunction with subjects such as psychology and sociology at the University of Strasbourg. In the late 1920s, he travelled to Freiburg, Germany, where he studied under the likes of Husserl and Heidegger. In 1930 Levinas was granted French citizenship. In the same year, his doctoral thesis was published — a text credited with introducing phenomenology to Jean-Paul Sartre. The outbreak of World War II saw Levinas drafted into the French army. He served as an interpreter until his capture in June 1940. Despite being a Lithuanian Jew by birth, he was interned in a military prison camp where he endured forced labour. As an officer in the French army, he was spared the fate that befell his immediate family, most of whom were murdered by the Nazis. The memory of the Nazi horror dominates much of Levinas' work.

Although sometimes nuanced, labyrinthine and, at times, seemingly contrived to frustrate rather than facilitate meaning, Levinas' philosophy is clearly governed by one core idea: a deep-seated pacifism. Levinas argues that Western philosophy is wedded to a counter-ethical process of conflict; this radical idea underpins his first magnum opus, *Totality and Infinity* (1961). This treatise opens with a discussion of war — an all-encompassing, as well as literal term for conflict. Levinas states that it is the Western preoccupation with the truth that generates this conflict. In short, if one is able to apprehend the truth, one is essentially self-sufficient or 'total'. Yet, as Levinas argues, this reassuring sense of totality is disastrous for it harbours an underlying antagonism towards others who are liable to challenge one's authority. Thus conceived, war is produced by a mobilisation of absolutes or subjective truths; within the ensuing *mêlée*, the trial by force becomes what Levinas terms, 'the test of the real'. He traces this conception of totality back to the teachings of Socrates and Plato. According to classical authority, the self is, as it were, self-contained — it is able to hold or comprehend the truth. For Levinas, this spirit of autonomy was perpetuated in the work of philosophers as diverse as Plotinus and Hegel.

To avoid this tide of thought, Levinas turned his attention to the structure of subjectivity. Husserl's influence can be seen here. For Levinas, the value of Husserlian phenomenology lay in the fact that it gave priority to the apperceptive or self-reflexive subject. To elaborate, phenomenology did not merely question *what is*. On the contrary, by way of a process of radical and obstinate self-reflection, it also inquired: 'How *is* what is?' With this question in focus, Levinas argued that, far from being self-sufficient or total, the self can only exist through reference to the non-self. In short, self-knowledge presupposes the existence of a power infinitely greater than oneself. Consciously echoing Cartesian thought, Levinas thus suggests that the subject is indebted to the idea of infinity. Opposing the work of many other continental philosophers, he thereby reinstates the subject — a subject which encounters itself through the mediation of an-Other; such an encounter preceding the disastrous desire for truth. Crucially, however, the encounter between the self and the Other is always passive. In slightly different terms, one welcomes the Other as the measure of one's own Being. It would seem to follow that one's subjectivity depends upon a non-aggressive or non-violent interface. Given its passive nature, Levinas concludes that this interface amounts to a proto-ethical moment which, by transcendental necessity, precedes all other ethical discourse. It is in this way Levinas undercuts traditional ethical debate.

A key and much-debated idea in *Totality and Infinity* is the notion of the *face* or *visage*. Levinas argues that the subject — an individuated subject that is able to enter into discourse — has always already presented themselves without being the content of an-Other; in essence, they have presented themselves as a *face*. But what exactly is this *face*? It is certainly one of the best-known ideas set out in *Totality and Infinity*, but it is also indefinite, vague, and even perplexing. As Susan Handelman has suggested, Levinas' 'notion of the face is often quite ambiguous and subject to varying definitions which are more like networks of associations than any precise stipulations'. Further, the very notion of the *face* appears to be based upon a paradox. To avoid mere abstraction, a veridical encounter with an-Other is necessary, and yet the *face* Levinas invokes is also elusive; it is not the human face *per se*.

Hence it is that for those accustomed to the rigours of analytic philosophy, Levinas' work can seem to lack clarity. As the example of the *face* illustrates, he does not appear to define key terms beyond a series of vague associations and analogies. But to a greater extent, this lack of clarity is necessary for Levinas is trying to transcend what he regarded as the irons of Western thought. Indeed, for Levinas, the art of the military commander, the *polemarch*, is comparable to that of the polemicist — ultimately, both beget war or *polemos*. Nevertheless, in 1964 Jacques Derrida published an essay in which he explored the extent to which Levinasian thought was still bound to the Western tradition and its implicit ethos of conflict. Levinas' rejoinder was *Otherwise than Being or Beyond Essence* (1974), a complex reconfiguration of his earlier work, composed in the (absent) light of post-structural concerns.

Therein, Levinas employs textual tactics that both impede passive consumption and bring to the fore the physical actuality of the printed word. Prolix compound sentences also coexist with a surfeit of aphorisms. The text can thus be construed as both vertiginous and claustrophobic. Such disparate play is designed to hinder any sedimentation in analytic clarity. Levinas also casts off much of his earlier terminology, adopting a new vocabulary which is far more fluid. As Étienne Feron points out, this new vocabulary 'ceaselessly interrupt[s] itself' as one posited term is substituted for another. This process of fluid substitution prevents any sense of conceptual stasis. In the few cases where Levinas does employ what appear to be key terms, they are usually paradoxical or at least somewhat enigmatic. The recurrent phrase *pre-original* is a case in point. One is left to ponder what it is that can precede 'the origin which nothing can (by definition) precede?'

To draw a parallel with the work of James Joyce, if *Totality and Infinity* can be compared to the nuanced and multifaceted novel *Ulysses*, *Otherwise than Being* is more akin to *Finnegan's Wake*, a text often lauded as one of the most challenging in the Western canon. *Otherwise than Being* is an attempt to philosophise at the very limits of language and conceptual thought. It is an often-perplexing work of playful profundity which both demands and charms, if, that is, one has the fortitude to read it. In his attempt to say what he believed must be said and what, at the same time, cannot be said, Levinas created a work of 'dissonant harmony' which is as much a performance piece as it is a work of academic philosophy.

***

Food for thought:

- What, if anything, is the precondition of our Being?
- Are we, at root, pacifists despite the glaring evidence to the contrary?
- What is the nature of Otherness and how does it shape who and what we are?
- Is our subjective Being dependent upon others? And if so, in what sense?
- How do we react to obscurity in writing? Is it a sign of pretence and/or charlatanism? Or is there a sense in which obscure excess can impart far more than a clipped and polished syllogism?
- Do we sometimes need to take a step back in order to step forward?
- Instead of asking, 'What is?' is it profitable to ask: 'How *is* what is?'
- Does the philosophical search for truth entail conflict?
- How do we judge the absolutes that others proffer?
- Is there a Truth or are there truths? Why might we seek either?
- Can 'philosophy' itself be undercut by ethics? Is a primordial love of the Other a prerequisite for the love of wisdom?
- Is *to be* to have already let be?

CHAPTER X

Jalal al-Din Rumi: The Extinction of the Soul

"You are not a drop in the ocean. You are the entire ocean in a drop."

In reply to Polonius' question, 'What do you read, my lord?' Hamlet famously quips, 'Words, words, words.' Within this exchange is the central paradox which lies at the heart of Rumi's poetry and philosophy; how are our worldly words to breach the veil of linguistic convention and reveal that which *lies* beyond? As Rumi puts it at the end of one of his lyrical poems, 'This is how it always is when I finish a poem. A great silence overcomes me, and I wonder why I ever thought to use language'. To cite another example: 'These words I'm saying so much begin to lose meaning: existence, emptiness, mountain, straw: words and what they try to say swept out the window, down the slant of the roof'. Yet despite this linguistic scepticism, Rumi's poetic output was truly prolific; he wrote thousands of lyrical poems or *ghazals* and his didactic *Masnavi* runs into six books of poetry and totals some 50,000 lines. Not without controversy, the latter work has been referred to as 'the Qur'an in Persian'.

Rumi was born in Balkh, northern Afghanistan, in September 1207. At the time of his birth, Balkh was within the Persian Empire; thus, to Afghanis and Persians, Rumi is Jalal al-Din Muhammad Balkhi. With the Mongol armies threatening to invade and, perhaps, with more localised religious tensions brewing, his family emigrated to Konya, Anatolia (now a city in central Turkey). The Roman for Anatolia is *Rum*—hence Jalal al-Din's surname. Rumi's father, Bahauddin Walad, was a theologian, religious teacher and mystic preacher who, in his *Maarif*, detailed his own visionary experiences and purported union with God. When he died in 1231, it fell to one of his disciples to further immerse Rumi into the teachings of Sufi piety. Travelling to Aleppo and Damascus, Rumi deepened his knowledge of the 'religious sciences' and upon his return to Konya, he took over the leadership of his late father's religious school. The gifted young scholar matured into something of an authority regarding religious matters and all seemed in place for a settled life of pious teaching and intellectual adherence.

However, in the Autumn of 1244, the beat changed. Rumi encountered a wandering mystic or dervish, an encounter which served to transform Rumi from a sober scholar of staid piety into an ecstatic philosopher-poet who was wont to whirl in public, a seeming microcosm of the celestial spheres themselves. The wandering dervish he met was Shams of Tabriz. The scholar and the dervish became inseparable. For a year and a half, what has been characterised as a mystical love ensued. Yet the true nature of what the two spiritual interlocuters shared is a mystery: 'Ask nothing more about Tabriz's Sun!' Rumi asserts. Such intense insularity generated friction. No doubt Rumi's family and disciples felt neglected and resentful. Sensing this growing tension, Shams left Konya. The dervish's disappearance was the catalyst for Rumi's transformation into a mystical philosopher-poet: 'In my hand there was always the Koran — Now I seized the lute out of love! In my mouth there were always words of laud — Now it is poetry and quatrains, and songs...' As reports began to arrive that Shams was in Syria, Rumi sent his son, Soltan Valad, to Damascus to entreat the dervish to return, and return he duly did. However, in December 1248, a year or so after his return, Shams disappeared for good. Tradition has it that he was murdered by Rumi's own disciples; some accounts even implicate another of Rumi's sons. In a state of seeming denial, Rumi travelled to Damascus seeking news of his friend. As reality dawned, he eventually discovered Shams within himself, setting this confluence within a broader mystical universality thus: 'Why should I seek? I am the same as he. His essence speaks through me. I have been looking for myself!'

When we hyphenate the philosopher and the poet, we necessarily end up creating something of a contradiction — a mixture that will not settle however much we stir the pot. Rumi was certainly not a systematic thinker in the mould of Aristotle, a figure of huge importance within medieval Islamic thinking. Indeed, the influential tenth-century philosopher, al-Farabi, is often referred to as the Second Teacher with Aristotle being cited as the First. However, Rumi does not express himself through the sobriety of syllogisms and other such logical constructs. Appealing to the many rather than the intellectual elect, he employs poetic analogies and didactic stories which entice and entertain instead of proselytising with premises and conclusions. In other words, his approach is not one of direct communication; he approaches us at a tangent. In this way, in place of stone-set ideas or deducted truths, he gives 'voice' to esoteric experiences and insights. In short, if we set aside Descartes' use of such terms for a moment, Rumi's work *works* through the application of 'intuition' rather than reason.

This distinction can be contextualised within the differences between the philosophical approaches of al-Kindi (*c.*801–873) and al-Ghazali (*c.*1058–1111). Al-Kindi, an Iraqi polymath, forged Neo-Platonism and Aristotelian logic into an amalgam conjoining Greek philosophy and Islamic theology, with reason driving epistemic progress. In his *Incoherence of the Philosophers*, al-Ghazali challenged this use of 'demonstrative proof' by the *falâsifa* or Arabic philosophers. Whilst not wholly disavowing the utility of Aristotelian logic, he prioritised intuition rather than reason. As he put it: 'Great is the difference between knowing the definition, the causes, and the conditions of drunkenness and actually being drunk! As to the definition and theory of drunkenness, the drunken man knows nothing, yet he is drunk; whereas the sober man, knowing the definition and the principles of drunkenness, is not drunk at all'. Similarly, Rumi did not disavow rational philosophy, but he did regard it as somewhat lacking in key respects. In terms reminiscent of Plato, he makes a distinction between knowledge and opinion, likening knowledge to a two-winged bird: 'Knowledge has two wings. Opinion has one wing: Opinion is defective and curtailed in flight'. Although perhaps resembling it in some sense, opinion is the opposite of reason he argues. But unlike Plato, Rumi holds knowledge to be inferior to vision and/or spiritual intuition: 'Know that knowledge is a seeker of certainty, and certainty is a seeker of vision and intuition'. Herein, Rumi's schema shows the limitations of rational philosophy and scholastic theology. At the limits of ontological insight, he suggests, such reasoning falters and thereby becomes an impediment to spiritual growth and transcendental love: 'Far-sighted reason — I have tested it. Henceforth, I'll make myself demented!'

Sufism itself can be characterised as the esoteric aspect of Islam; rather than looking unto fulfilling the Laws and thereby aspiring to a state of blessedness *post-mortem*, the inward path supposedly facilitates a direct access to a state of eternal union within which the ego dissipates. In this manner, the Sufi mystic aspires to a state within which one's narrow sense of selfhood is extinguished or annihilated (*al-fana*) — to die before one dies as it were. But such a death is in actuality a union or an 'extinction' *with* unity, a unity with the divine. Rumi likens such a state to being a drop of water becoming aware of itself as part of the ocean: 'You are not a drop in the ocean. You are the entire ocean in a drop'. However, this is not an appeal to a form of pantheism; instead, unity implies a continuity at a higher spiritual level:

'The colour of iron is lost in the colour of the fire, the iron has assumed the colour of the fire but is [nonetheless] iron'.

Perhaps one of the most well-known depictions of this state of unity and severance can be found in the exordium or prologue to Book One of *The Masnavi* — that is to say, in *The Song of the Reed*. The image of the reed can be associated with the musicality of mystical dance in terms of the plaintive play of the reed-flute or *ney*. Moreover, the poet's words might be said to flow from the reed-pen itself. In both instances, the reed acts as a medium for the expression of mystical unity. And yet, having been torn from the reed-bed, the reed-flute in the prologue laments its state of separation — a severance which is representative of 'each human's agony' whilst alienated from divine unity. The suggestion is, however, that it is only through an awaking to such severance that one can become aware of one's spiritual alienation and thereby enact recourse. Or metaphorically, the reed must be uprooted in order to express the reality of a lost unity, which, in relation to God, the mystical path seeks to recuperate. One might argue that such images of subjectivity and objectivity imply a duality inimical to the envisaged absolute unity. However, what Rumi is postulating is an extinction or annihilation of the self-concept and an attendant subsistence of the soul *with* God. In this way, the rationally conceived 'I' is replaced by an 'I' which is implicitly non-individualistic. From within the terms of another of Rumi's images, the divine needle cannot accommodate the split thread of ontological egoism: 'Now you are I, please enter in this place, because for two I's here there isn't space'. In this sense, life constitutes a journeying back to God for Rumi — symbolically, the reed returning to the bed from whence it was torn.

In opposition to hard-nosed empirical determinists such as Paul Rée and likewise countering the unabashed libertarianism of philosophers such as Jean-Paul Sartre, Rumi offers what might be termed a nuanced intervention in the free will debate. Within the Muslim theology of the tenth-century CE, a schism of sorts arose regarding the issue of determinism or *jabr* ('compulsion') and the notion of free will. Set within the idea that an omnibenevolent God cannot cause evil, the Mutazilites argued that humans are essentially free agents, hence the existence of evil. On the other hand, the Asharites argued that it is only God that has causal efficacy; consequently, as philosophers such as Malebranche would later argue, a leaf cannot fall from a tree unless God decrees it so. In his *Masnavi*, Rumi engages this heated debate at a tangent, offering narrative commentaries which do not harden into dogma. In one such instance, he narrates a debate between a lion and its prey; the lion's prey offering arguments for an acceptance of fatalism or divine determinism. Precautions cannot prevent what God decrees they avow. This idea is further illustrated through a story within which a nobleman in Solomon's court conspires to outrun Azrael, the Angel of Death. So as to elude his fate, the nobleman appeals to Solomon to have him magically carried by the wind to India's southern tip. However, unbeknownst to the nobleman, this is the divinely allotted place of his death: 'All of the world's affairs are planned this way, [...] To flee from God? That's simply laughable!' But having offered such illustrations of fatalism or determinism, Rumi advances counter-positions. For example, the lion declares that 'effort also is the Prophet's way' invoking the hadith: 'Trust God, but still make sure your camel's tied!' Another memorable counter comes in the form of a ladder: 'The lion said, "But God has caused to rise a ladder right before our very eyes; we must climb rung by rung to the top — it's selfish to resign to fate and stop"'. In contrast to the Asharite theologians, such examples seek to show that human effort or volition is not wholly illusory. As Rumi puts it in Book Three of *The Masnavi*, 'On Judgement Day, free will's the skill that's judged!' And yet, as illustrated by the example of the nobleman, Rumi is also aware of the deterministic or fatalistic consequences of an appeal to an omniscient God that can annul human agency by decree. Although by no means a reasoned argument for a form of compatibilism, what Rumi does offer is the elusive idea that the truth might well lie somewhere between the polarities of free will and determinism; a position that might be said to counter the *principium tertii exclusi*. Couched in Rumi's own terms, God gives our acts their being 'for they're His creation' and yet our acts are 'God's manifestation'. In this way, God creates human actions, and humans *acquire* or elect them; thus, predestination or divine determinism is maintained, whilst, at the same time, human agency and responsibility are said to remain intact. Rumi concedes that when we think within these terms, we must embrace what he likens to a 'backward-and-forward-at-once vision' — a vision wherein we must somehow square the apparent oppositions of divine action and human volition. Flying in the face of Aristotelian logic, Rumi states plainly that what he is proffering 'is not rationally understandable'. Yet for a mystical thinker, rather than negating its validity, such a concession might be said to underscore its wisdom. Indeed, within terms that could be said to playfully echo Plato's cave myth, Rumi likens the approach of the Asharite logicians to that of a fly in donkey's urine; upon its straw boat, the fly imagines itself upon a boundless sea. Unpacking the moral, Rumi concludes, 'Narrow interpretations are like this fly, with straw and urine they falsify'.

Rumi's poetry has been translated into many languages and he has been lauded as one of the most popular poets in the USA. His love poetry has been performed by Hollywood luminaries such as Madonna, Demi Moore and Goldie Hawn and he was the librettist for *Monsters of Grace*, a multimedia opera by the influential American composer and pianist, Philip Glass. The

English singer and songwriter, Chris Martin, included a reading of Rumi by Coleman Barks in one of his *Coldplay* tracks. In fact, it is Coleman Barks who has been instrumental in popularising Rumi's poetry through his best-selling translations; although, as he neither reads nor writes Persian, Barks' renderings are more akin to creative interpretations, drawing as they do on earlier translations. And herein resides an issue: arguably, the popularity of Rumi via such re-workings is complicit with decoupling the original verse from its Islamic context through what amounts to an act of spiritual colonialism. One need only read the Barks 'translation' as tattooed on the actor Brad Pitt's arm to see such spiritual colonialism at play — ink under the skin expunging all traces of the original Islamic context.

***

Food for thought:

- What are the limitations of words?
- As Rumi puts it, 'Have you ever plucked a rose from R.O.S.E?'
- Is philosophy tantamount to a protracted word game?
- In the words of the philosopher Jacques Derrida, is there anything beyond the text?
- Is there a form of intuitive knowledge which transcends rational insight?
- In its Aristotelian guise, is philosophy wedded to the play of binary oppositions and a Greek lexicon which unduly delimits intuitive insight?
- Contrary to Max Stirner, is the idea of a unified and self-sufficient ego erroneous?
- Is a schism in thought or faith always divisive?

- To what extent is a passage through a state of alienation (antithesis) a necessary means to higher (synthetic) understanding?
- Without invoking the problematic compatibilism of philosophers such as Hume and Hobbes, might there be an alternative means by which to navigate the Scylla and Charybdis of freedom and determinism?
- Is the act of translation always a re-creative act?
- Can a reimagining of an earlier translation really be deemed a 'translation'?
- To what extent is Rumi's popularity in the West complicit with an act of spiritual colonialism?

Author Article List

Selected content developed from articles first appearing in the following publications (in date order).

Harvey, Lawrence (2003). 'Emmanuel Levinas.' *The Philosophers' Magazine*. Issue 21. 1st Quarter. p. 53.

— (2004). 'Emmanuel Levinas.' *Great Thinkers: A-Z*. Julian Baggini & Jeremy Stangroom (eds.). Continuum Press: London. pp. 144–146.

— (2005). 'Max Stirner.' *The Philosophers' Magazine*. Issue 29. 1st Quarter. pp. 80–1.

— (2006). 'T. E. Hulme.' *The Philosophers' Magazine*. Issue 33. 1st Quarter. pp. 80–1.

— (2009). 'Clive Bell.' *The Philosophers' Magazine*, Issue 44. 1st Quarter. pp. 94–6.

— (2016). 'Nicolas Malebranche.' *The Philosophers' Magazine*. Issue 73. 2nd Quarter. pp. 54-7.

— (2020). 'Paul Rée, Nietzsche, and the Myth of Libertas.' *Liberal Arts: Thinking Now and Then*. Available at: https://liberalarts.org.uk/paul-ree-nietzsche-and-the-myth-of-libertas/

— (2021). 'J. W. Dunne.' *The Philosophers' Magazine*. Issue 93. 2nd Quarter. pp. 44–7.

— (2022). 'Wherein Lies the Value of Art? Clive Bell's Radical Aesthetic Vision.' *Liberal Arts: Thinking Now and Then*. Available at: https://liberalarts.org.uk/wherein-lies-the-value-of-art-clive-bells-radical-aesthetic-vision/

Selected Bibliography

Works listed under the same name are alphabetised by title.

Max Stirner

Clark, John P. (1976). *Max Stirner's Egoism*. London: Freedom Press.

Camus, Albert (1967). *The Rebel*. Anthony Bower (trans.). Harmondsworth: Penguin.

Levenson, Michael H. (1995). *A Genealogy of Modernism*. Cambridge University Press.

Marx, Karl & Frederick Engels (1976). *Collected Works*. Clemens Dutt, W. Lough & C. P. Magill (trans.). Vol. 5. London: Lawrence & Wishart.

McLellan, David (1969). *The Young Hegelians and Karl Marx*. New York: Praeger.

Newman, S. (2011). *Max Stirner*. Palgrave Macmillan: Basingstoke and New York.

Paterson, R. W. K. (1993). *The Nihilistic Egoist: Max Stirner*. Aldershot: Gregg Revivals.

Read, Herbert (1949). *Existentialism, Marxism and Anarchism: Chains of Freedom*. London: Freedom Press.

Stirner, Max (2000). *The Ego and Its Own*. Steven Tracy Byington (trans.). Cambridge: Cambridge University Press.

J. W. Dunne

Broad, C. D. (1935). 'Mr. Dunne's Theory of Time in *An Experiment with Time*.' *Philosophy*. 10.38, pp. 168–85.

Dunne, J. W. (1927). *An Experiment with Time*. A & B Black: London.

— (1940). *Nothing Dies*. Faber & Faber: London.

— (1934). *The Serial Universe*. Faber & Faber: London.

Priestley, J. B. (2000). *An Inspector Calls and Other Plays*. Penguin Books: London.

— (1964). *Man and Time*. Aldus Books: London.

Stewart, V. (2008). 'J. W. Dunne and Literary Culture in the 1930s and 1940s'. *Literature and History*. 17.2, pp. 62–81.

Sullivan, J. W. N. (1927). [Anon review]. 'Dreaming of the Future'. *Times Literary Supplement*, September 29, p. 659.

Wells, H. G. (1927). 'Explorations in the World of Dreams'. *New York Times*, July 10, p. 3.

— (2005). *The Shape of Things to Come*. Penguin Books: London and New York.

Donna Haraway

Bell, David and Kennedy, Barbara M. (eds.) (2001). *The Cybercultures Reader*. Routledge: London and New York.

Haraway, Donna (2001). 'A Cyborg Manifesto: Science, technology and socialist-feminism in the late twentieth century.' In David Bell and Barbara M. Kennedy (eds). *The Cybercultures Reader*. Routledge: London and New York. pp. 291–324.

— (2004). "Cyborgs, Coyotes, and Dogs: A Kinship of Feminist Figurations" and "There are Always More Things Going on Than You Thought! Methodologies as Thinking Technologies." *The Haraway Reader*. Routledge: London and New York. pp. 321–41.

— (2000). *How Like a Leaf: An Interview with Thyrza Nichols Goodeve*. Routledge: New York and London.

— (1988). 'Situated Knowledges: The Science Question in Feminism and the Privilege of Partial Perspective.' *Feminist Studies*. 14:3, pp. 575–99.

Kafer, Alison (2013). *Feminist, Queer, Crip*. Indiana: Indiana University Press.

Orr, Jackie (2012). 'Materializing a Cyborg's Manifesto.' *Women's Studies Quarterly*. 40.1/2, pp. 273–80.

Young, Robert M. (1992). 'Science, Ideology and Donna Haraway.' *Science as Culture*. 15.3, pp. 165–207.

T. E. Hulme

Bergson, Henri (1913). *An Introduction to Metaphysics*. T. E. Hulme (trans.). London: Macmillan and Co.

Browning, W. R. F. (1947). 'T. E. Hulme.' *Church Quarterly Review* 145, pp. 59–65.

Ferguson, Robert (2002). *The Short Sharp Life of T. E. Hulme*. London: Allen Lane.

Hulme, T. E. (1911). [Pseud. Thomas Gratton]. 'Bergson Lecturing.' *The New Age* 10.1, November 2, pp. 15–16.

— (1912). "The Complete Poetic Works of T. E. Hulme." *The New Age*. 10.13, January 25, p. 307.

— (1955). *Further Speculations*. Sam Hynes (ed.) Minneapolis: University of Minnesota Press.

— (1911). 'Mr. Balfour, Bergson, and Politics.' *The New Age*. 10.2, November 9, pp. 38–40.

— (1913). 'Mr. Epstein and the Critics.' *The New Age*. 14.8, December 25, pp. 251–3.

— (1916). 'Note Book.' *New Age*. 18.10, January 6, pp. 234–5.

— (1960). *Speculations*. Herbert Read (ed.) London: Routledge and Kegan Paul.

— (1915). 'The Translator's Preface to Sorel's "Reflections on Violence."' *The New Age*. 17.24, October 14, pp. 569–70.

Jones, A. R. (1960). *The Life and Opinions of Thomas Ernest Hulme*. London: Victor Gollancz.

Krieger, Murray (1953). 'The Ambiguous Anti-Romanticism of T. E. Hulme.' *ELH: A Journal of English Literature*. 20.4, pp. 300–14.

Roberts, Michael (1982). *T. E. Hulme*. Manchester: Carcanet New Press.

Nicholas Malebranche

Doxsee, Carll Whitman (1916). 'Hume's Relation to Malebranche.' *The Philosophical Review*. 25.5, pp. 692–710.

Malebranche, Nicolas (1997). *Dialogues on Metaphysics and on Religion*. Nicholas Jolley and David Scott (eds.). David Scott (trans.). Cambridge University Press: Cambridge and New York.

— (1997). *The Search after Truth: With Elucidations of The Search after Truth*. Thomas M. Lennon and Paul J. Olscamp (eds.). Thomas M. Lennon (trans.). Cambridge University Press: Cambridge and New York.

— (1992). *Treatise on Nature and Grace*. Trans. Patrick Riley. Clarendon Press: Oxford.

Nadler, Steven (ed.) (2000). *The Cambridge Companion to Malebranche*. Cambridge University Press: Cambridge and New York.

Schmaltz, Tad M. (2010). 'Malebranche and Leibniz on the Best of All Possible Worlds.' *The Southern Journal of Philosophy*. 48.1, pp. 28–48.

Paul Rée

Andreas-Salomé, L. (1990). *Looking Back: Memoirs*. Breon Mitchell (trans.). Ernst Pfeiffer (ed.). New York: Paragon House.

Critchley, S. (2020). *Tragedy, the Greeks and Us*. London: Profile Books.

Rée, P. (2003). *Basic Writings*. Robin Small (trans.). Urbana and Chicago: University of Illinois Press.

— (1973). 'Determinism and the Illusion of Moral Responsibility'. Stefan Bauer-Mengelberg (trans.). In Edwards, P. & Pap,

A. (eds.) *A Modern Introduction to Philosophy: Readings from Classical and Contemporary Sources*. London: Freedom Press, pp. 10–27.

Sartre, J-P. (1993). *Existentialism & Humanism*. Philip Mairet (trans.). London: Methuen.

Small, R. (2005). *Nietzsche and Rée: A Star Friendship*. Oxford: Oxford University Press.

Sophocles. (1974). *The Theban Plays: King Oedipus, Oedipus at Colonus, Antigone.*. E. F. Watling (trans.). London: Penguin Books.

Clive Bell

Bell, C. (2007). *Art*. New York: Dodo Press.

Collingwood, R. G. (1958). *The Principles of Art*. Oxford: Oxford University Press.

Fishman, S. (1963). *The Interpretation of Art*. Berkeley & Los Angeles: University of California Press.

Fry, R. (1914). 'A New Theory of Art'. In Bullen, J. B. (ed.) (1988). *Post-Impressionist England*. London: Routledge, pp. 487–91.

Fry, R. (1923). *Vision and Design*. London: Chatto and Windus.

Lawrence, D. H. (1936). 'Introduction to these Paintings.' In Edward D. McDonald (ed.) (1961). *Phoenix: The Posthumous Papers of D. H. Lawrence.* London: William Heinemann.

Marcus, L. (2014). 'Bloomsbury Aesthetics'. In Rosner, V. (ed.) *The Cambridge Companion to the Bloomsbury Group*. Cambridge: Cambridge University Press, pp. 162–80.

McLaughlin, T. M. (1977). 'Clive Bell's Aesthetic: Tradition and Significant Form.' *The Journal of Aesthetics and Art Criticism*. 35.4, pp. 433–43.

Plato (1987). *The Republic*. Desmond Lee (trans.). London: Penguin Books.

Rosenbaum, S. P. (2003). *Georgian Bloomsbury: Volume 3: The Early Literary History of the Bloomsbury Group, 1910–1914.* Basingstoke: Palgrave McMillian.

Warburton, N. (1995). *Philosophy: The Basics.* London & New York: Routledge.

Warburton, N. (2006). *The Art Question.* London & New York: Routledge.

Wittgenstein, L. (2006). *Philosophical Investigations.* G. E. M. Anscombe (trans.). Oxford: Blackwell Publishing.

Zeki, S. (2013). 'Clive Bell's "Significant Form" and the neurobiology of aesthetics'. *Frontiers in Human Neuroscience.* 7:730. Available at: https://doi.org/10.3389/fnhum.2013.00730

Princess Elisabeth of Bohemia

Broad, Jacqueline (2002). *Women Philosophers of the Seventeenth Century.* Cambridge: Cambridge University Press.

Descartes, René (1968). *Discourse on Method and The Meditations.* F. E. Sutcliffe (trans.). London: Penguin Books.

Ebbersmeyer, Sabrina and Hutton, Sarah (eds.) (2021). *Elisabeth of Bohemia (1618–1680): A Philosopher in her Historical Context.* Dordrecht: Springer.

Janssen-Lauret, Frédérique (2018). 'Elisabeth of Bohemia as a Naturalist Dualist.' In *Early Modern Women on Metaphysics.* Emily Thomas (ed.). Cambridge: Cambridge University Press. pp. 171–87.

Princess Elisabeth of Bohemia and René Descartes (2007). *The Correspondence between Princess Elisabeth of Bohemia and René Descartes.* Lisa Shapiro (ed. and trans.) Chicago: University of Chicago Press.

Rorty, Amélie Oksenbery (ed.) (1986). Essays on Descartes' *Meditations.* Los Angeles and London: University of California Press.

Schmaltz, Tad M. (2009). 'Descartes on the Extensions of Space and Time'. *Analytica* 13.2, pp. 113–47.

Shapiro, Lisa. (2021). 'Elisabeth, Princess of Bohemia.' *The Stanford Encyclopedia of Philosophy*. Autumn Edition. Edward N. Zalta (ed.). Available at: https://plato.stanford.edu/archives/fall2021/entries/elisabeth-bohemia/.

— (2021). 'Princess Elisabeth and the Challenges of Philosophizing.' In S. Ebbersmeyer and S. Hutton (eds.) pp. 127–44.

— (2019). 'Princess Elisabeth of Bohemia as a Cartesian.' In *Oxford Handbook of Descartes and Cartesianism*. Tad Schmaltz and Steven Nadler (eds.). Oxford: Oxford University Press. pp. 287–302.

— (1999). 'Princess Elisabeth and Descartes: The Union of Mind and Body and the Practice of Philosophy.' *British Journal for the History of Philosophy*. 7.3, pp. 503–20.

Tomoko, L. Kitagawa (2021). 'Passionate Souls: Elisabeth of Bohemia and René Descartes.' *The Mathematical Gazette: A Journal of the Mathematical Association*. 105.563, pp. 193–200.

Emmanuel Levinas

Bernasconi, Robert & Wood, David (eds.). (1998). *The Provocation of Levinas: Re-thinking the Other*. London: Routledge.

Critchley, Simon (1992). *The Ethics of Deconstruction: Derrida and Levinas*. Edinburgh: Edinburgh University Press.

Critchley, Simon & Bernasconi, Robert (eds.). (2002). *The Cambridge Companion to Levinas*. Cambridge: Cambridge University Press.

Davis, Colin (1996). *Levinas: An Introduction*. Cambridge: Polity Press.

Derrida, Jacques (1995). Interview with Richard Kearney. 'Deconstruction and the other.' Richard Kearney (ed.).

States of Mind: Dialogues with Contemporary Thinkers. New York: New York University Press, pp. 156–76.

— (1997). *Writing and Difference*. Alan Bass (trans.). London: Routledge.

Feron, Étienne (1992). *De l'idée de transcendance à la question du langage: L'Itinéraire philosphique d'Emmanuel Levinas*. Grenoble: Jerôme Millon.

Handelman, Susan A. (1991). *Fragments of Redemption: Jewish Thought and Literary Theory in Benjamin, Scholem, and Levinas*. Bloomington & Indianapolis: Indiana University Press.

Levinas, Emmanuel (1999). *Alterity and Transcendence*. Michael B. Smith (trans.). London: The Athlone Press.

— (1998). *Collected Philosophical Papers*, Alphonso Lingis (trans.). Pittsburgh: Duquesne University Press.

— (1985). *Ethics and Infinity*. Richard A. Cohen (trans.). Pittsburgh: Duquesne University Press.

— (1989). *The Levinas Reader*. Seán Hand (ed.). Oxford: Blackwell.

— (1998). *Otherwise than Being or Beyond Essence*. Alphonso Lingis (trans.). Pittsburgh: Duquesne University Press.

— (1996). *Totality and Infinity: An Essay on Exteriority*. Alphonso Lingis (trans.). Pittsburgh: Duquesne University Press.

Jalal al-Din Rumi

Abou-Bakr, O. (1994). 'Abrogation of the Mind in the Poetry of Jalal al-Din Rumi.' *Alif: Journal of Comparative Poetics*. 14. pp. 37–63.

Ali, R. (January 5, 2017). 'The Erasure of Islam from the Poetry of Rumi.' *The New Yorker*. Available at: https://www.newyorker.com/books/page-turner/the-erasure-of-islam-from-the-poetry-of-rumi

Baldock, J. (2004). *The Essence of Sufism*. Royston: Eagle Editions.

Burckhardt, T. (2008). *Introduction to Sufi Doctrine*. Bloomington: World Wisdom.

Chittick, W. (2000). *Sufism: A Short Introduction*. Oxford: Oneworld Publications.

Iqbal, A. (1983). *The Life and Work of Jalal-ud-Din Rumi*. London: Octagon.

King, J. R. (1989). 'Narrative Disjunction and Conjunction in Rumi's "Mathnawi."' *The Journal of Narrative Technique*. 19:3, pp. 276–86.

Lewis, F. D. (2000). *Rumi Past and Present, East and West: The Life, Teachings and Poetry of Jalâl al-Din Rumi*. Oxford: Oneworld Publications.

Mojaddedi, J. A. (2012). *Beyond Dogma: Rumi's Teachings on Friendship with God and Early Sufi Theories*. Oxford: Oxford University Press.

Ridgeon, L. V. J. (ed.) (2014). *The Cambridge Companion to Sufism*. Cambridge: Cambridge University Press.

Rumi, J. (2000). *Love is a Stranger: Selected Lyric Poetry of Jelaluddin Rumi.* Kabir Edmund Helminski (trans.). Boston: Shambhala.

— (2008). *The Masnavi: Book. 1.* Jawid Mojaddedi (trans.). Oxford: Oxford University Press.

— (2004). *Rumi: Selected Poems*. Coleman Banks (trans.). London: Penguin Books.

Schimmel, A (1988). 'Mystical Poetry in Islam: The Case of Maulana Jalaladdin Rumi'. *Religion & Literature*. 20:1, pp. 67–80.

IFF
BOOKS

ACADEMIC AND SPECIALIST

Iff Books publishes non-fiction. It aims to work with authors and titles that augment our understanding of the human condition, society and civilisation, and the world or universe in which we live. If you have enjoyed this book, why not tell other readers by posting a review on your preferred book site.
Recent bestsellers from Iff Books are:

Why Materialism Is Baloney
How true skeptics know there is no death and fathom answers to life, the universe, and everything
Bernardo Kastrup
A hard-nosed, logical, and skeptic non-materialist metaphysics, according to which the body is in mind, not mind in the body.
Paperback: 978-1-78279-362-5 ebook: 978-1-78279-361-8

The Fall
Steve Taylor
The Fall discusses human achievement versus the issues of war, patriarchy and social inequality.
Paperback: 978-1-78535-804-3 ebook: 978-1-78535-805-0

Brief Peeks Beyond
Critical essays on metaphysics, neuroscience, free will, skepticism and culture
Bernardo Kastrup
An incisive, original, compelling alternative to current mainstream cultural views and assumptions.
Paperback: 978-1-78535-018-4 ebook: 978-1-78535-019-1

Framespotting
Changing how you look at things changes how
you see them
Laurence & Alison Matthews
A punchy, upbeat guide to framespotting. Spot deceptions and
hidden assumptions; swap growth for growing up. See and be free.
Paperback: 978-1-78279-689-3 ebook: 978-1-78279-822-4

Is There an Afterlife?
David Fontana
Is there an Afterlife? If so what is it like? How do Western ideas
of the afterlife compare with Eastern? David Fontana presents the
historical and contemporary evidence for survival of
physical death.
Paperback: 978-1-90381-690-5

Nothing Matters
a book about nothing
Ronald Green
Thinking about Nothing opens the world to everything by
illuminating new angles to old problems and stimulating new
ways of thinking.
Paperback: 978-1-84694-707-0 ebook: 978-1-78099-016-3

Panpsychism
The Philosophy of the Sensuous Cosmos
Peter Ells
Are free will and mind chimeras? This book, anti-materialistic but
respecting science, answers: No! Mind is foundational
to all existence.
Paperback: 978-1-84694-505-2 ebook: 978-1-78099-018-7

Punk Science
Inside the Mind of God
Manjir Samanta-Laughton
Many have experienced unexplainable phenomena; God, psychic abilities, extraordinary healing and angelic encounters. Can cutting-edge science actually explain phenomena previously thought of as 'paranormal'?
Paperback: 978-1-90504-793-2

The Vagabond Spirit of Poetry
Edward Clarke
Spend time with the wisest poets of the modern age and of the past, and let Edward Clarke remind you of the importance of poetry in our industrialized world.
Paperback: 978-1-78279-370-0 ebook: 978-1-78279-369-4

Readers of ebooks can buy or view any of these bestsellers by clicking on the live link in the title. Most titles are published in paperback and as an ebook. Paperbacks are available in traditional bookshops. Both print and ebook formats are available online. Find more titles and sign up to our readers' newsletter at
www.collectiveinkbooks.com/non-fiction
Follow us on Facebook at
www.facebook.com/CINonFiction